Fire-King
An Information and Price Guide

Joe Keller & David Ross

Schiffer Publishing Ltd
4880 Lower Valley Road, Atglen, PA 19310 USA

Dedication

This book is dedicated to Winfield and Ruthie Foley, for their support, understanding, and deep appreciation of this project.

Designed by Bonnie M. Hensley
Cover design by Bruce M. Waters
Type set in Humanst521 BT

ISBN: 0-7643-1641-9
Printed in China
1 2 3 4

Published by Schiffer Publishing Ltd.
4880 Lower Valley Road
Atglen, PA 19310
Phone: (610) 593-1777; Fax: (610) 593-2002
E-mail: Schifferbk@aol.com
Please visit our web site catalog at **www.schifferbooks.com**
We are always looking for people to write books on new and related subjects. If you have an idea for a book please contact us at the above address.

This book may be purchased from the publisher.
Include $3.95 for shipping.
Please try your bookstore first.
You may write for a free catalog.

In Europe, Schiffer books are distributed by
Bushwood Books
6 Marksbury Ave.
Kew Gardens
Surrey TW9 4JF England
Phone: 44 (0) 20 8392-8585; Fax: 44 (0) 20 8392-9876
E-mail: Bushwd@aol.com
Free postage in the U.K., Europe; air mail at cost.

Contents

Acknowledgments

We would like to thank many people who helped with *Fire-King, An Information and Price Guide*. Their generosity has made the undertaking of this project possible.

Dixie Hardesty was a tremendous help at the photo shoot at Jeff Snyder's Minneapolis home. Her knowledge, enthusiasm, and interest in Fire-King was a tremendous asset. What to photograph? What to include in each shot? What was important? What to do next? Dixie and all the other Fire-King aficionados present at the photo shoot in Minneapolis always had the answers!

The kindness and time given by Joe and Anna Thomas and Karen and Allen Mowery was such a great contribution. The miles logged in traveling to Minneapolis and the time spent wrapping all of their Fire- King treasures to be photographed is greatly appreciated.

We are very grateful to Jeff Snyder who was instrumental in convincing all of his Fire-King friends to help us out and share the combined wealth of their collections. If that wasn't enough, Jeff turned his home in to a "Fire-King Collectors' Hotel" for almost a week and trusted us with his enormous collection. "Whatever you need!" was the most often heard comment from our very generous host. Jeff's hospitality made our work in Minnesota a complete pleasure.

The time given and Fire-King shared with us by Kellie Davison, Mark and Angela Ebertowski, George and Rena Mead,and Billie Rhodes was a welcome addition to the seemingly never ending supply that we already had to work with at Jeff Snyder's home.

Dixie and Randy Hardesty were once again a great help both in organizing the photo shoot in Lancaster, Ohio and for loaning us Fire-King catalogs. Thanks to Shane Hardesty for his help, understanding, and support.

Molly J. Allen, Jane Bohlen, and John and Theresa Mitchell were once again on hand to help us out in Lancaster and loaned treasures from their collections. It seems like just yesterday that we had all gathered at the home of Jane and Jerry Bohlen for a photo shoot for our first book, *Jadite, An Identification and Price Guide*.

Ed and Pat Gietzen, Jim Heft, Walt and Betty Marquart, and Verylean and Dick Summers were all helpful with the Lancaster Ohio photo shoot. Thank you to all of the collectors and Fire-King enthusiasts who gave so much of themselves and shared their Fire-King with us.

Jeffrey B. Snyder and Douglas Congdon-Martin worked long hours and never complained during photo shoots. It was a pleasure working with Jeffrey and Doug once again! Thanks also to Team Schiffer for all of the help and support along the way.

Special thanks to David Daley,Scott Differ, and Ruthie and Winfield Foley.

Foreword and Organization

Fire-King dinnerware and kitchenware has become an extremely popular collectible in recent years. We felt that an introductory book was needed that presented the subject matter in a simple and straightforward manner – the way that a beginning collector or enthusiast might collect. To do this we have decided to organize the book by color. This was, after all, how most of the items were marketed. Thus, a Jadite Splash Proof mixing bowl is located with Jadite, not with mixing bowls.

This book includes items produced by Anchor Hocking Glass Co. as part of their Fire-King lines. It also includes items produced by this company that seem consistent with these lines, but which may not have been strictly marketed as "Fire-King." The word "Fire-King" was not consistently used in company advertising or on products. It is therefore impossible to see "Fire-King" as a well-defined category. Rather, it is a grouping of oven-safe kitchenware and dinnerware that was marketed for both home and institutional use.

We did not consider all Anchor Hocking glass to be "Fire-King." Patterns produced by Anchor Hocking that did not fit with their Fire-King lines have not been included. Similarly, many institutional lines and common crystal items have not been included because of limitations of space and interest.

The table of contents delineates the basic organization of the book. Please consult the index for specific patterns.

Introduction

Anchor Hocking Glass Corporation was created in 1937 by the merger of Anchor Cap and Closure Corporation and the Hocking Glass Company. This brought together mass production and colored glassware. The word "Fire-King" first appears on glassware in the early 1940s. Intended as a group of oven-proof lines, "Fire-King" became the most successful of Anchor Hocking's products.

The earliest Fire-King was the Philbe dinnerware line, introduced in 1940. In 1942, this was transformed into the Sapphire Blue oven-ware, which, along with Jadite, became the signature items of the Fire-King line. The oven-ware was attractive, durable, and inexpensive. The dinnerware was bold, attractive, and multi-purpose. Items were multi-function. A casserole was used to bake, serve, and then store leftovers in the refrigerator. Many pieces were produced that did not have a specific function – like utility trays, bakers, and covered loaf pans. These pieces were marketed in various ways, with the goal being to see each piece as multi-functional.

Fire-King's Jadite lines have become the most popular in recent years. Produced both for home and institutional use, Jadite has inaccurately become synonymous with "Fire-King" in popular consciousness. Not all Jadite is Fire-King and clearly not all Fire-King is Jadite. But Jadite's popularity has definitely affected the collectability of other Fire-King. Prices of Jadite have risen dramatically in recent years. Pieces that were difficult to sell 10 years ago are expensive today. The high prices of Jadite have brought attention to many of the other Fire-King lines. While there have always been Fire-King collectors, this new wave of interest since the Jadite fad, has greatly increased the number of Fire-King enthusiasts.

In 1976, Anchor Hocking stopped producing their Fire-King lines, or at least stopped using the Fire-King logo on most of its pieces. Many items, however, were simply produced without the Fire-King logo and remain in production today. Similarly, Anchor Hocking's failed attempt to reissue Jadite in 2000, further presents the difficulty of collecting a product whose manufacturer is still in existence.

Fire-King batter pitchers.

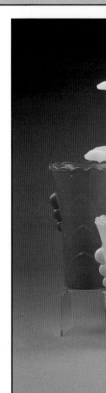

Fire-King kitchenware.

Pricing

Establishing prices for Fire-King has been extremely difficult. The antiques/collectibles marketplace has been especially difficult to analyze since the introduction of the Internet. Seemingly rare items no longer appear as difficult to locate as once thought, while common items seem so prevalent that they appear as almost unsaleable. The highly visible nature of the Internet brings many rare items to the marketplace. However, the super-high prices that a small group of advanced collectors may be willing to pay usually cannot be sustained. In many of the recent books that have included Fire-King, prices have reflected these very high and very visible prices that a small group were once willing to pay. This has begun to settle down and many of the most rare pieces have resurfaced in the marketplace only to be sold at a fraction of their previous "value."

Fire-King is mostly mass-produced glassware. Since many Fire-King lines were produced through the 1970s and many moulds remain active at Anchor Hocking, value and rarity are often impossible to discern. We have relied on our own observation of the marketplace to establish values – at shows, shops, and on-line. Currently not all Fire-King is marketable. We have observed sets of Fire-King at seemingly reasonable prices that simply will not sell because of color, fashion, trends, etc. We have tried to reflect prices that can be realized in today's marketplace.

To establish prices, we have contacted leading collectors and dealers of Fire-King and kitchenware. We have also watched and recorded prices in national publications, at shows, and on the Internet. Ultimately, the prices presented in this book are our best assessment of current trends as we see them. Like all authors of "price guides," these prices reflect the limitations of our experience.

Jadite ball jug.

Ribbed leftovers.

Jadite

Alice 9 1/4" dinner plate, $35-40, cup and saucer, $10-12.

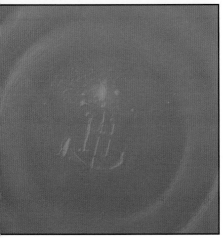

Anchor Hocking backstamp found on some Alice dinner plates.

The popularity of Jadite in recent years has been remarkable. First created by the McKee and Jeannette Glass Companies in the 1930s, Anchor Hocking produced several lines of Jadite kitchen and dinnerware from the 1940s to 1970s.

Most Depression Glass dealers have dealt in the earlier Jadite kitchenware for years, but until recently, Jadite dinnerware was largely ignored as a collectible. Jane Ray, which is especially popular today, was rarely in demand a decade ago. Several factors have played a role in this "craze" phenomenon, including fashion color trends, Martha Stewart's kitchen set, and several features in national Home magazines.

The prices for Jadite have finally begun to settle after years of escalation, especially on the more expensive pieces. A group of hard-core collectors had driven the prices of many of the super-rare items to unheard of levels. Many pieces have sold for in excess of $10,000. but those days seem to be over. Basic dinnerware is still in demand, though supply has been able to keep up with demand on most pieces. After all, most of this dinnerware was mass-produced for over 20 years.

Backstamp of Alice dinner plate with Fire-King logo. Rare.

Three Band dinner plate, $1000+, 8"
vegetable, $125-150.

Two Band chili bowl, $400-500.

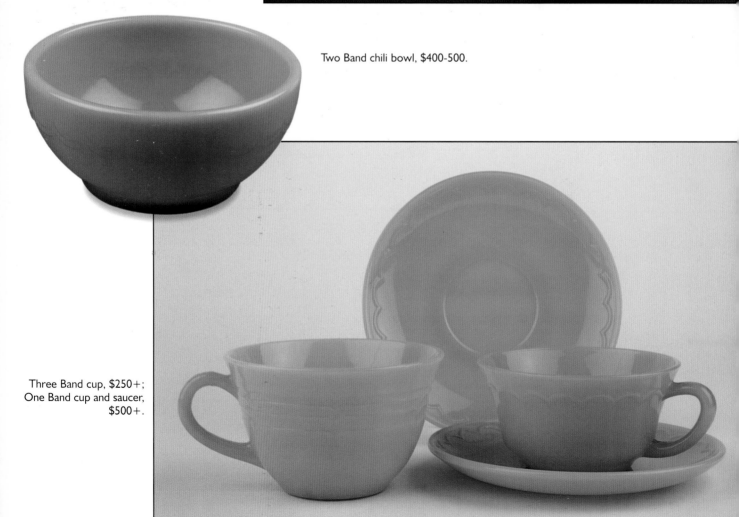

Three Band cup, $250+;
One Band cup and saucer,
$500+.

10

Charm dinnerware.

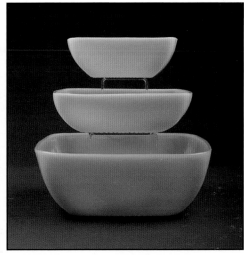

Charm bowls. 4 3/4" dessert, $15-18; 6" soup, $60-65; 7 3/8" salad bowl, $65-75.

Charm sugar, $20-22; creamer, $20-22.

Charm cups and saucers, $12-15. Add $3-5 for original labels.

Charm 11" x 8" platter, $75-85.

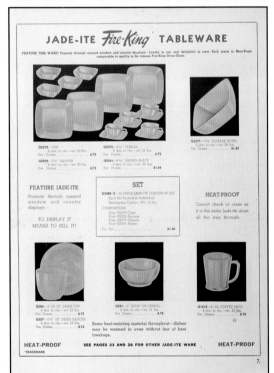

Charm plates. 9 1/4" dinner, $60-65; 8 3/8" lunch, $20-22; 6 5/8" salad, $40-45.

Fire-King catalog advertisement for Charm dinnerware.

Jane Ray dinnerware.

Jane Ray bowls. Clockwise from back right: rare flanged soup, $500-550; 8 1/4" vegetable, $30-35; 7 5/8" soup, $20-25; 5 7/8" cereal, $20-25; 4 7/8" dessert bowl, $10-12.

Jane Ray plates. 9 1/8" dinner, $15-18; 7 3/4" salad, $12-15; 6 1/4" bread and butter, $125-150. The bread and butter plate is extremely scarce. Most of these have been found in Canada.

Pages from catalogs.

Jane Ray 12" x 9" platter, $30-35.

Jane Ray cups and saucers. Regular cup and saucer, $8-10; demitasse cup and saucer, $90-100. There are two styles of regular saucers: plain and rayed. The rayed is slightly more scarce.

Jane Ray covered sugar, $30-35; creamer, $15-18.

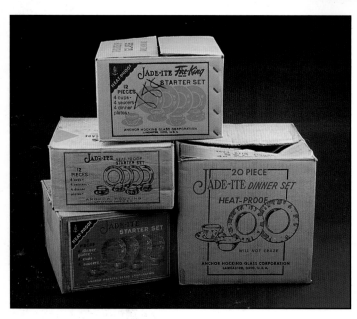

Original boxes for Jane Ray, $25-75. Condition and graphics greatly affect their value.

Jane Ray dinner with Niagara Falls painting, $40-45; regular 8 oz. mug with Niagara Falls painting, $45-50.

Jane Ray dinner plate made into a clock. These are currently being made and sell for $25-50.

Original magazine ad for Jane Ray and other Fire-King dinnerware.

Photo from Anchor Hocking "morgue." 10 3/8" plate marked "1949." Very rare, $1000+.

Restaurantware plates. 9" dinner plate, $20-25; 8" lunch plate (scarce), $40-50; 6 3/4" pie plate, $10-12; 5 1/2" bread and butter plate, $12-15.

Restaurantware grill plates. With or without tabs, $22-25 each.

Five-part grill plate, $40-50.

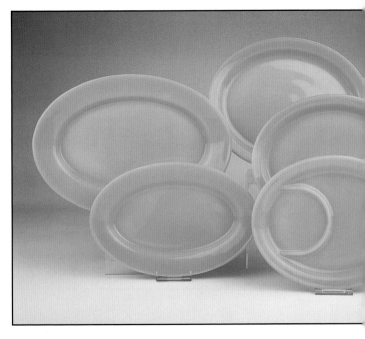

Restaurantware platters: 9 1/2" oval, $50-55; 11 1/2" oval, $55-60; 9 3/4" football, $60-70; 8 7/8" small football, $90-100; 8 7/8" partitioned, $75-85.

Restaurantware bowls. Clockwise from top: 9" rim soup, $100-125; 8 oz. cereal with flanged lip, $25-30; chili bowl (technically not part of Restaurantware line), $12-15; 10 oz. bowl with beaded rim, $30-35; 4 3/4" fruit, $12-15; 15 oz. bowl with beaded rim, $30-35.

Handled soup cup and saucer
(rare), $750-1000.

Restaurantware demitasse cup
and saucer, $90-100.

Restaurantware cups and
saucers: Tall cup/saucer,
$15-18; regular cup/
saucer, $12-15; flared
cup/saucer, $30-35;
demitasse cup/saucer,
$90-100.

Restaurantware mugs:
extra large, $22-25; slim
chocolate, $28-30;
medium mug, $20-22.

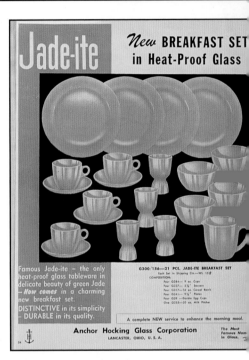

Restaurantware brochure.

Advertisement
for breakfast set.

Breakfast set. Cup and saucer,
$12-15; 1700 line 9 1/8"
dinner, $25-30; milk pitcher,
$85-95; eggcup, $35-40;
breakfast bowl, $90-100.

1700 line. 6" cereal,
$45-50; flat soup, $50-
60; dinner plate, $25-3
cup and saucer, $12-15

18

Ransom cup and saucer (left), $20-25; regular 1700 line cup and saucer (right), $12-15.

Breakfast bowls. Plain, $90-100; with red ivy, $100-125.

Sheaves of Wheat dinner plate, $80-100; bowl, $100-125; cup and saucer, $80-100.

Close-up of the design on the Sheaves of Wheat dinner.

Shell dinnerware. 13" platter, $75-85; 10" dinner, $22-25; 7 1/4" salad plate, $15-18; cup/saucer, $15-18; creamer, $25-30; sugar bowl base, $20-25; sugar lid, $45-50; 8 1/2" vegetable, $30-35; 7 5/8" soup plate (not shown), $35-40; 6 3/8" cereal, $20-25; 4 3/4", $12-15.

Shell tid-bit trays. These were produced after they left the factory. $50-75 each.

Swirl dinner plate, $85-95.

Oval vegetable. Rare, $500-750. This piece does not strictly match Shell, but has been put with this pattern by collectors. Not mentioned in company literature as being produced in Jadite.

Jadite child's plate, $1000-1200.

Swirl cup and saucer, $75-85.

Swirl platter, $1000+.

Comparison of Shell cup and saucer
(left) and Swirl cup and saucer
(right).

Child's mug, $400-500.

Beaded-edge mixing bowls. The largest is extremely rare in Jadite. 4 7/8", $20-25; 6", $20-25; 7 1/4", $25-30; 8 3/8", $400-600.

Colonial mixing bowls. 6", $100-125; 7 1/4", $100-125; 8 3/4", $125-150. White with fired-on green band, $35-40.

Ribbed mixing bowls. 4 3/4" (scarce), $100-125; 5 1/2", $40-45; 7 1/2", $55-65.

Ribbed bowls with crystal covers. 5 1/2",
$45-50; 4 3/4", $110-135.

Splash Proof mixing bowls. The smallest bowl is extremely rare.
6 3/4" one-quart, $500-600; 7 1/2" two-quart, $50-60; 8 1/2"
three-quart, $100-125; 9 1/2" four-quart, $125-150.

Splash Proof bowls with white floral decals.
Scarce, $300-500 each.

Splash Proof mixing bowls with red floral
decals. Scarce, $300-500 each.

Swedish Modern mixing bowls. Also called teardrop bowls. The two middle sizes are the most difficult to locate. Measurements indicate the width of bowl. 5" one-pint, $65-75; 6" one-quart, $175-200; 7 1/4" two-quart, $165-175; 8 3/8" three-quart, $135-150.

Swirl mixing bowls. The smallest is quite scarce. 5", $175-200; 6", $25-30; 7", $25-30; 8", $25-30; 9", $35-40.

Catalog page for mixing bowls.

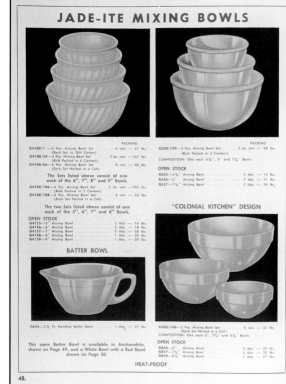

Odd translucent 6" mixing bowl. Unusual, $100-125.

Original store display for free Swirl mixing bowls with the purchase of flour. Rare, $300-500.

Saucepans. One spout, $100-125; two spout, $150-175. These pieces can be found with a variety of original labels. Label adds $25-50 to value.

1 1/2" quart casserole. Very rare in Jadite, $2500-3000. Gravy pitcher. Rare, $2000-2500.

Jadite custards. From top: large custard with Philbe design, $200-250; ruffled custard, $300-400; custard with beaded-edge, $65-75.

Jadite pieces with ivory Sweetheart set. Jadite pie plate, $250-300; loaf pan 5"x 9", $65-75; large baking dish 6 1/2" x 10 1/2", $800-1000.

Philbe pie plate, $450-500; plain pie plate, $250-300; with rolling pin made by McKee, $750-1000. A very good reproduction of the rolling pin was available from Martha Stewart in 2000 that retailed for around, $65.

Philbe decorated Jadite. Pie plate, $450-500; 5" x 5" leftover, $35-40; 5" x 10" leftover, $75-85; decorated mug, $125-150; plain mug with same foot as Philbe mug, $25-30; custard, $200-250.

Large original label for pie plate. Adds $75-100 to value.

Refrigerator dishes were sold individually and as a 3-piece set. 5" x 5", $35-40; 5" x 10", $75-85.

Crystal covered leftovers. 4"x 4", $30-35; 4"x 8", $50-60.

Jadite butter dishes. Rear: rare ribbed butter, $500+; front: crystal covered butter, $125-150. The crystal covered butter was one of the pieces that Anchor Hocking attempted to produce for their Fire-King 2000 line. Beware of reproductions.

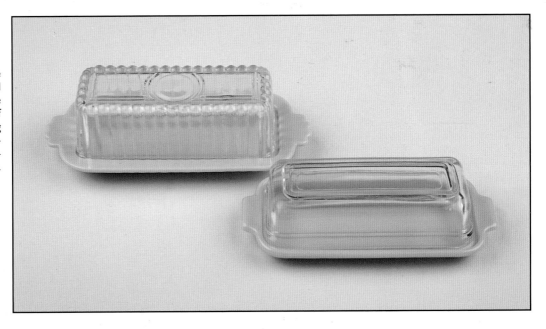

Close-up of mugs.

From left: 3" individual bean pot, $500+, flared custard, $200-250; rolled custard, $200-250.

Clockwise from left: 6 1/2" x 10 1/2" baking dish, $800-1000; 4 1/2" handled casserole, $600-750; ruffled custard, $300-400; 5" crystal covered French casserole, $450-500; custard, $65-75; 5" flanged bowl, rare, $400-500.

Swirl pitcher, $3000-4000.

Manhattan pitcher, $3500-4500.

Jadite ball jugs. Manhattan, $3500-4000; Swirl, $3000-4000; Puro advertising jug, $1500-1800; plain ball jug, $650-750. The plain ball jug was to be included in the Fire-King 2000 reproduction line. Beware of reproductions.

Very rare target ball jug, $4000-5000.

Fire-King batter pitchers, $50-60. Labels add $10-25. Two different styles of batter pitchers are found. One has a 3/4" band, the other has a 1" band. The 1" band pitchers are slightly scarcer and sell for $10 more.

Close-up of batter bowl label.
"Only 39 cents."

Tulip-covered shakers, $75-85 pr.; tulip covered grease jar, $45-50. Prices for items with lids in excellent condition.

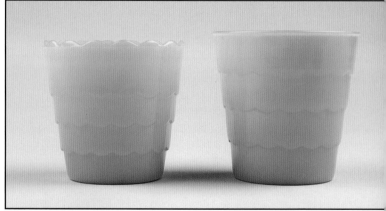

Bottoms of rare Jadite candy dishes, $200-300 each.

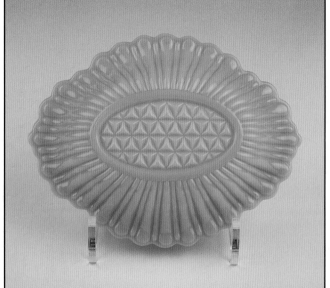

Jadite flower pots. Scalloped edge, $25-30; smooth edge, $20-25.

Unusual Jadite candy dishes, $200-300 each.

Art Deco vase, $20-25.

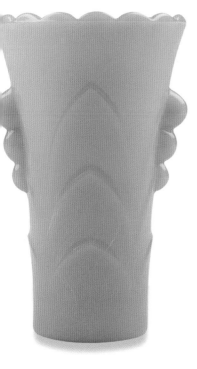

Leaf candy dish, $20-25. This piece is found with several different labels. Labels add $5-15.

Sea Shell dessert bowl or candy dish, $25-30. With label add $10-20.

Covered ribbed candy, $75-100. These are almost impossible to find in mint condition. Price should reflect the extent of the damage, especially on the points of the cover.

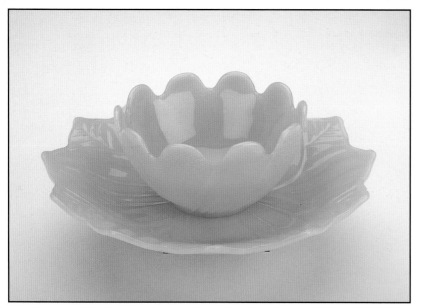

Leaf and Blossom set. Leaf plate, $20-25; blossom bowl, $20-25.

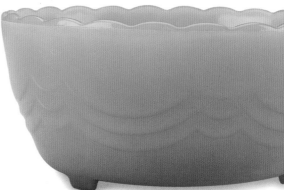

Jadite bulb planter, $25-30.

Jadite rose-covered jewel box, $65-75; fired-on green with white cover, $25-30.

Jadite chili bowl with cottage cheese advertising cover, $65-75. This cover is unusual in that it mentions "Fire-King."

Chili bowl with advertising cover, $30-35.

Chili Bowl with Heinz Soups advertising in red on side. Scarce, $75-100.

Smooth edge flower pot advertising cover for cottage cheese, $35-40.

D-handled mug with floral decoration and the name Dora, $25-30. This is vintage lettering, but was done after the mug left the factory.

Jadite souvenir mugs, $30-40 each.

Set of 4 D-handled mugs in original packaging, $75-100.

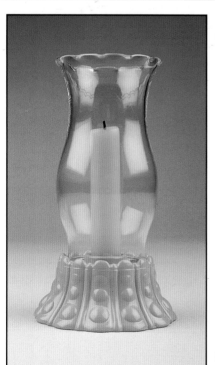

Jadite items used to make a tidbit tray, lamp, and clock.

Scarce hurricane lamp, $125-150.

Opaque Blues: Azurite and Turquoise Blue

Charm dinnerware. Back row from left: platter, $25-30; 9 1/4" dinner, $18-20; 8 3/8" lunch, $10-12; 6 5/8" salad plate, $12-15. Middle row: 7 3/8" salad bowl, $30-35; 6" soup bowl, $18-20; sugar, $12-14; creamer, $12-14; cup and saucer, $5-7. Front: 4 3/4" dessert bowl, $8-10.

"Azur-ite" label adds $2 to value of piece.

Azurite and Turquoise Blue have a growing number of enthusiasts. This dinnerware is still affordable and available. Azurite is a very soft white/blue found in the popular Charm (square) dinnerware. Turquoise Blue is bolder with a deeper, richer color.

Blue Kitchenware is also extremely popular, especially the Splash Proof and Swedish Modern mixing bowl sets – and they are only one third the price of their Jadite counterparts. The batter bowl, which is one of the most frequently seen pieces of Jadite, is rarely seen in blue.

We have been consistently selling these lines to our Japanese customers. Fire-King is very popular (and expensive) in Japan.

Novelty salad plate. Decorated after the piece left the factory, $20-25.

Swirl dinnerware. Back row: Platter, $18-20; 9" flanged soup, $75-100; cup/saucer, $5-7; 7 3/8" salad plate, $5-8; covered sugar, $10-12. Front: 8 1/4" vegetable, $20-22; 5 7/8" cereal, $15-18; 9" dinner plate, $10-12; 4 7/8" dessert bowl, $8-10; 7 5/8" flat soup, $12-15; creamer, $10-12. Tumblers with dark blue rings were marketed with some sets, $5-8 each.

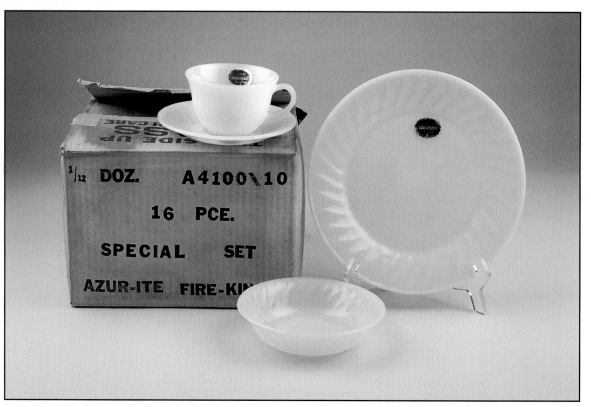

16-piece boxed set. Box adds $8-10.

Turquoise Blue dinnerware. Clockwise from left: creamer, $8-10; 10" dinner plate, $25-30; 9" lunch/dinner, $8-10; 7 1/4" salad plate, $10-12; 6" bread plate, $15-20; open sugar bowl, $10-12; cup/saucer, $5-7; 4 1/2" berry bowl, $8-10; 6 1/2" soup, $20-22; 8" vegetable, $20-25. A variety of Anchor Hocking glass was sold with large sets, $5-10 each.

Comparison of flanged soup on left with the flat soup on right. The flanged soup is very scarce.

Metal tidbit rack that holds 6", 7", and 10" plates. Rack only, $20-25.

Turquoise Blue label. Adds $2-3.

Decorated 18-piece boxed set. Box adds $20-25.

Turquoise Blue boxed snack sets. These boxes are fairly common, $15-20. 9" snack plate with cup ring, $6-8.

Basketweave bowl, $90-100; berry bowl, $8-10; chili bowl, $10-12; odd size bowl, $30-35.

Left: batter pitcher, scarce, $500-600. D-handled mug, $10-12

Bowls with metal accessories. Azurite mixing bowl/ice tub, $50-60; Turquoise Blue vegetable casserole, $30-35. Some metal holders are marked "Italy" on bottom.

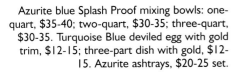

Azurite blue Splash Proof mixing bowls: one-quart, $35-40; two-quart, $30-35; three-quart, $30-35. Turquoise Blue deviled egg with gold trim, $12-15; three-part dish with gold, $12-15. Azurite ashtrays, $20-25 set.

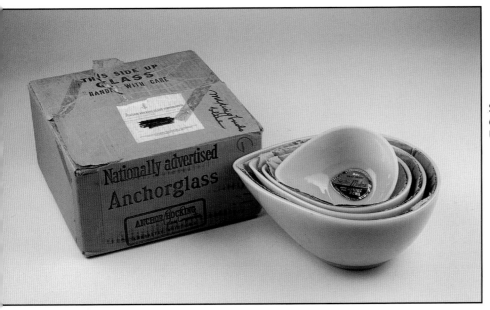

Swedish Modern mixing bowls: 5", $30-35; 6", $40-45; 7 1/4", $40-45; 8 3/8", $45-50. Undecorated original box, $15-20.

Back row from left: Azurite flowerpot, $18-20; chili bowl, $10-12; blossom bowl, $10-12. Front: crystal covered ribbed bowl, $40-50; breakfast bowl, $40-50.

Back row. Decorated chili bowls, $20-25. Front: red ivy breakfast bowl, $35-40; breakfast bowl, $40-50.

Sheaves of Wheat. Rare blue dinner plate, $750+.

40

Pink and Burgundy Dinnerware

Most of the pink dinnerware was made through a fired-on process that incorporates white glass with the pink as an over-spray. The obvious exception is the rarely seen Rose-ite, which is actually pink glass. Rose-ite is extremely scarce.

Demand for most pink dinnerware is moderate. This is still affordable glassware. While the supply is not as large as that of Jadite or Azurite, this glass can be found with a little searching.

The Banded Burgundy glass is extremely scarce and in heavy demand. This is the level of rarity that falls into the "name your price" category. There are enough collectors for these rare items to sustain the high prices and to continue their escalation.

Pink Swirl and Wrought Iron glassware. Pink Swirl: 11" round chop, $20-25; covered sugar, $12-15; creamer, $8-10; 7 1/4" round vegetable (scarce), $40-50; 8 1/4" round vegetable, $20-25. Wrought Iron: pitcher, $20-25; carafe, $15-20; glasses, $5-10.

Swirl dinnerware: dinner plate, $8-10; 7 3/8"
salad plate, $5-7; cup/saucer, $5-7; flat soup,
$12-15; 4 7/8" fruit bowl, $5-7. Go-along
range salt and pepper, $15-20 pr.

Decorated 12-piece
starter set. Box, $20-25.

Box for pink Swirl.
"Dinnerware for
Gracious Living." Box,
$8-10.

Wrought Iron glassware. Pitcher, $20-25; carafe, $15-20; glasses, $5-10.

Pink beaded-edge mixing bowls. 4 7/8", $50-60; 6", $30-35; 7 1/8", $30-35; 8 3/8", $45-50.

Boxed 19-piece set. Box, $10-15.

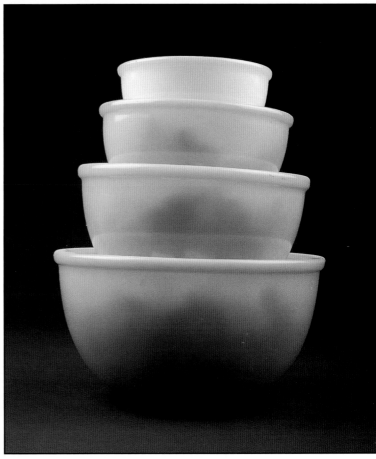

Rose-ite Swirl. All pieces scarce. Back row: 12" oval platter, $250-275; dinner plate, $100-125; salad plate, $80-100; round vegetable, $225-250. Front row: flat soup, $100-125; sugar, $125-150; creamer, $125-150; oval vegetable, $300-350; fruit bowl, $50-75; 2 1/4" footed sherbet, $65-75; cup/saucer, $75-100.

Rare Jadite oval vegetable, $500+; Rose-ite oval vegetable, $300-350.

Three Bands — Burgundy: dinner plate, $200-250; round vegetable, $300-350; 4 7/8" dessert, $100-150.

Burgundy Three Bands round vegetable, $300-350.

44

Ivory Dinnerware and Kitchenware

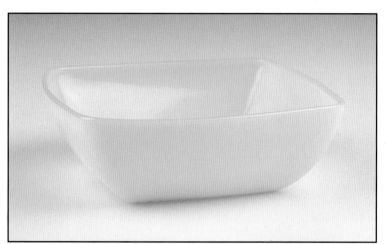

Charm 4 3/4" dessert bowl (scarce), $30-35.

There are numerous collectors for ivory but also a good supply at the moment. While rare pieces are commanding extremely high prices on the Internet, your basic dinnerware is often overlooked at your local flea market. Ivory looks great as a collection and is a bargain at today's prices. There should be more Charm ivory out there – very little has been found to date.

Ivory dinnerware can be found with numerous decorations. Some of these were done at the factory; many were done after leaving the factory. It is also important to realize that there is both ivory and ivory/white glassware. As the name implies, ivory/white is somewhere in between ivory and white glassware. It does not blend well with either color. Most collectors of ivory avoid mixing this color in their sets.

Ivory Kitchenware is much more of a challenge to accumulate. While Swirl bowls and small baking dishes are frequently seen, many of the other pieces are quite scarce. Gay Fad Studios decorated many ivory pieces – these pieces are highly sought after. Refer to the Gay Fad section of this book for more information.

Charm 8 3/8" lunch plate, $25-30.

Ivory dinner plate. Unknown pattern, $75-100.

Jane Ray: dinner plate, $20-25; cup/saucer, $15-20; 4 7/8" fruit bowl, $20-25; ribbed ivory 7 1/2" bowl, $25-30; 4 3/4" ribbed bowl, $20-25.

Laurel "ivory white:" 11" serving plate, $25-30; 9" dinner, $12-15; 7 3/8" salad plate, $8-10; 8 1/4" round vegetable, $30-35; 7 5/8" flat soup, $18-20; 4 7/8" dessert bowl, $8-10; sugar, $10-12; creamer, $10-12; cup/saucer, $8-10.

1700 line in Ivory: 12" platter, $25-30; 9" dinner plate, $7-9; 8 1/2" vegetable bowl, $30-35; 6" cereal bowl, $10-12; Ransom cup/saucer (front), $8-10; St. Denis cup/saucer (back) $6-8. Butter dish, ivory with crystal cover, $50-60.

Ivory boxed set. Notice the items from various lines. 1700 dinner plate, $7-9; chili bowl, $6-7; Ransom cup/saucer, $6-8; D-handled mug, $5-7. Box, $10-15.

Ivory Swirl. Clockwise from left. 8 1/4" vegetable bowl, $15-18; 6" cereal, $15-?0; 4 7/8" fruit, $5-7; 12" platter, $18-20; ?" dinner plate, $8-10; 7 3/8" salad plate, $5-7; covered sugar, $8-10; creamer, $6-?; cup/saucer, $5-7; footed sugar, $5-7; flat soup, $10-12.

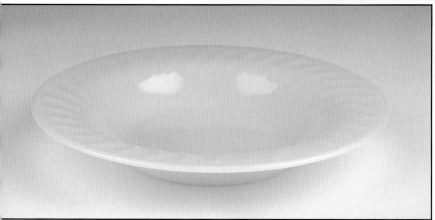

Swirl 9" flanged soup (scarce), $75-100.

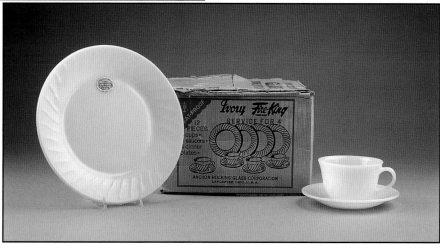

Boxed set of Ivory Swirl. Box, $10-15.

Swirl 11 7/8" serving plate, $25-30.

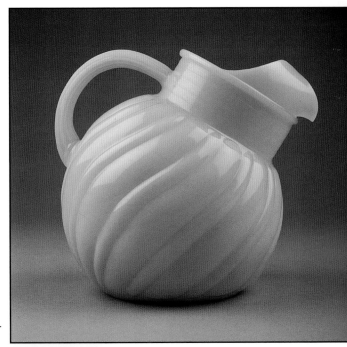

Ivory Swirl ball jug. Rare, $600-800.

Sunrise. Ivory Swirl with red trim. Clockwise from left: 8 1/4" vegetable, $20-25; 12" oval platter, $20-25; 9" dinner, $10-12; 7 3/8" salad, $8-10; covered sugar, $18-20; creamer, $10-12; cup/saucer, $8-10; 6" cereal, $18-20; go-along eggcup, $5-7; 7 5/8" flat soup, $15-18; 4 7/8" fruit, $5-7.

Plates decorated and handpainted after they left the factory, $20-25 each.

Golden Anniversary. Ivory Swirl trimmed with 22K gold. Back row: 12" platter, $8-10; 9" dinner, $4-6; 7 3/8" salad plate, $3-5; footed sugar, $4-6; footed creamer, $4-6. Front row: 8 1/4" vegetable, $8-10; 7 5/8" flat soup, $6-8; 4 7/8" fruit, $3-5; cup/saucer, $3-4.

Ivory Three Bands. 8 1/4" vegetable, $35-45; dinner, $12-15; cup/saucer, $10-15; 4 7/8" fruit, $8-10.

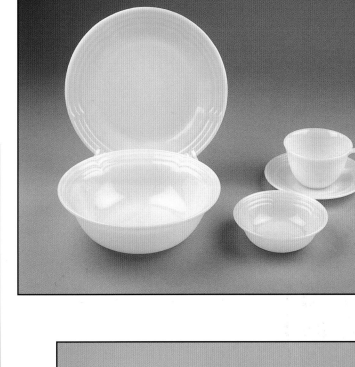

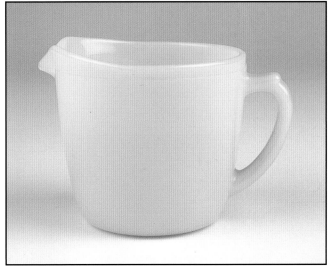

D-handled mug, $5-7.

Ivory 4000 line creamer (scarce), $20-25.

Restaurantware demitasse cups and saucers, $30-35 each set.

Ivory child's plate, $75-100. Child's mug, $40-50. This items are true ivory, not ivory/white as in the trimmed plates.

Children's plates, $30-35; circus chili bowls, $20-25. each.

Back row: shaving mug, $18-20; Jiminy Cricket mug, $20-25; Atwood's coffee mug, $10-12; chili bowl, $6-7; 8 oz. D-handled mug, $5-7. Front row: flower pot, $12-15; paneled cup, $20-25; 8 1/2 oz. mug, $8-10.

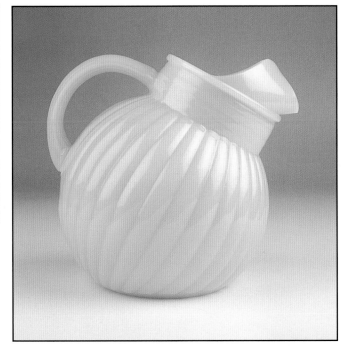

Ivory vertical ribbed, "Pillar" ball jug, $500-600.

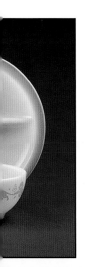

Sweetheart baking set. Covered 1 1/2-quart casserole, $15-20; flared 5 oz. custard, $3-4; loaf pan, 5" x 9 1/8", $10-12; 9" round cake, $15-20; baking pan, 6 1/2" x 10 1/2", $10-12; 9" pie plate, $8-10. Original box, $10-15.

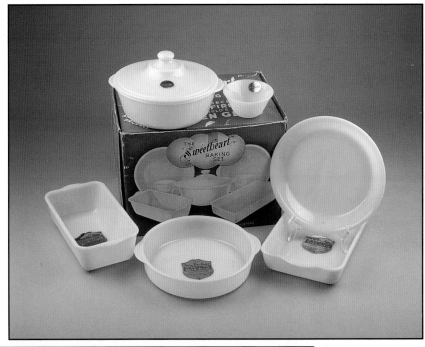

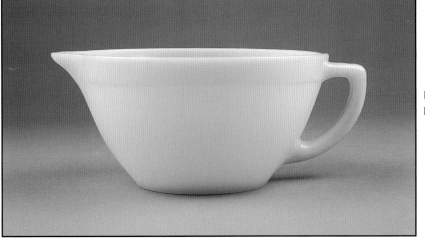

Ivory batter pitcher, $18-20.

Ovenware: two-quart casserole, $15-20; table server/stand for casserole, $8-10; one-pint casserole, $20-25. Custards/individual bakers from left: ruffled, $2-3; rolled, $4-5; flared, $3-4; tall, $4-5.

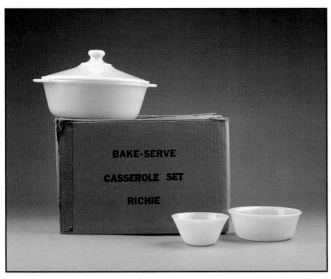

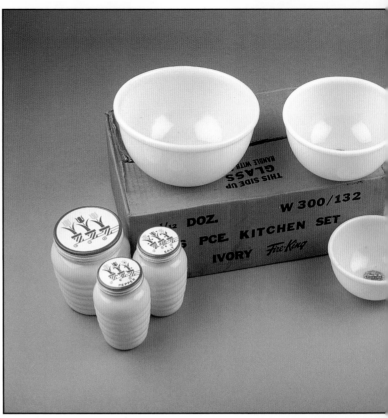

1-1/2 quart casserole, $15-20; flared custard, $3-4; 5 1/2" individual pie dish, $10-12.

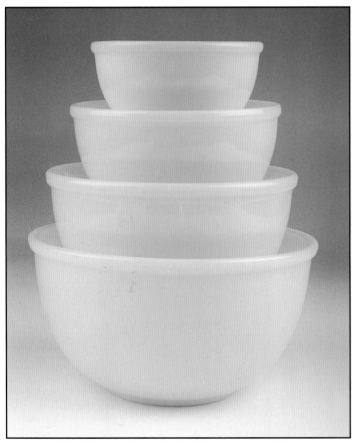

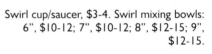

Swirl cup/saucer, $3-4. Swirl mixing bowls: 6", $10-12; 7", $10-12; 8", $12-15; 9", $12-15.

Beaded-edge mixing bowls: 4 7/8", $10-12; 6", $10-12; 7 1/8", $15-18; 8 3/8" (scarce), $50-65.

Leftovers with crystal covers. Ivory: 4" x 4", $6-8; 4" x 8", $8-10. Jadite: 4" x 4", $25-30; 4" x 8", $40-45. Original boxes, $5-10.

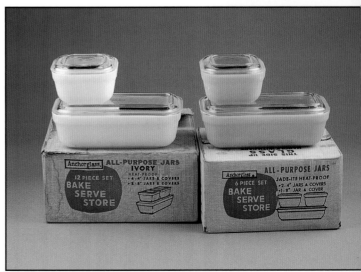

Ivory Kitchen set. Mixing bowls: 4 7/8", $10-12; 6", $10-12; 7 1/8", $15-18. Range salt and pepper with tulip lids, $40-45 set; grease jar with tulip lid, $22-25.

Splash Proof bowls: one-quart, $15-20; two-quart, $15-20; three-quart, $15-20; four-quart, $20-25. Range jar and cover, $20-25; range shakers with solid red lids, $25-30.

Decorated Kitchen set. Box, $12-15.

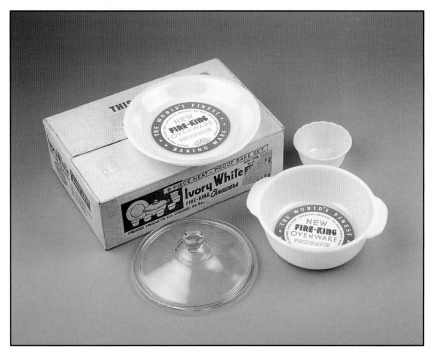

Ivory White bake set. One-quart casserole with crystal cover, $8-10; 8" pie plate, $6-8; ruffled custard, $2-3.

Original box for Ivory White
baking set, $5-10

Cover for Philbe one-quart casserole, $40-50.
Complete Philbe one-quart casserole (not shown),
$125-150. Bowls from left: individual pie, $10-12;
breakfast bowl, $30-35; straight-sided bowl, $15-20.

9" round cake with shield label, $15-20. Label adds $2-3.

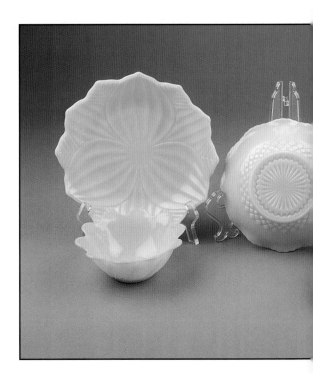

54

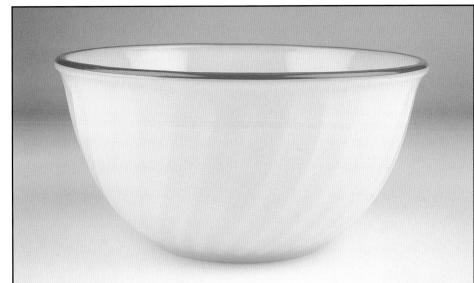

Swirl 9" mixing bowl with Sunrise red trim, $35-40

Ivory chili bowls with floral trim, $15-18; circus bowls, $20-25.

Loaf pans. Poppy, $25-40; Poinsettia, $40-50; Apple, $40-45.

Three-part candy dish, $20-22; Swirl mixing bowls with decals, $30-35 each; Gay Fad blue floral candy, $30-35.

Leaf plate, $12-15; blossom bowl, $8-10; Diamond candy dish, $12-15; footed comport, $15-18; experimental bowl, $50-75.

Peach Lustre

Peach Lustre refers to the orange iridescent glassware that is reminiscent of Carnival Glass. While there are some collectors who enthusiastically collect this glassware, the supply more than offsets the demand. The Kitchenware sells better for us than the dinnerware, especially mixing bowls and batter pitchers.

Lustre and Jadite breakfast pieces. Dinner plate, $10-12; milk pitcher, $45-50; breakfast bowl, $15-20.

Bubble bowls. 11" salad, $12-15; 8 1/2" large berry, $10-12; 5 1/4" cereal, $10-12; 4 1/2" berry, $10-12.

Peach Lustre advertisement.

Peach Lustre (Laurel) dinnerware. Back row: 9" dinner, $4-5; 7 1/2" salad plate, $2-3; cup and saucer, $4-5. Front: 7 1/2" soup plate, $5-7; 4 7/8" dessert, $3-4.

Original Peach Lustre boxed set. Box adds $10-15.

Peach Lustre 11" serving plate, $10-15; 8 1/2" round vegetable, $8-10; sugar, $4-5; creamer, $4-5.

Hand-painted green Laurel decoration on Peach Lustre cup, $8-10.

Royal Lustre dinnerware. Back row: 13" platter, $18-20; 10" dinner plate, $8-10; 7 3/8" salad plate, $4-5; covered sugar, $12-15. Front row: cup and saucer, $5-7; 6 3/8" cereal, $5-7; 5" dessert, $3-4; demitasse cup and saucer, $20-25; creamer, $6-8.

Royal Lustre flanged rim soup, $20-25.

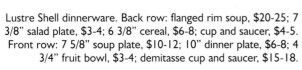

Lustre Shell dinnerware. Back row: flanged rim soup, $20-25; 7 3/8" salad plate, $3-4; 6 3/8" cereal, $6-8; cup and saucer, $4-5. Front row: 7 5/8" soup plate, $10-12; 10" dinner plate, $6-8; 4 3/4" fruit bowl, $3-4; demitasse cup and saucer, $15-18.

Lustre Shell three-tier tid-bit, $25-30; 13" platter, $18-20; 8 1/4" small platter, $25-30; 8 1/2" round vegetable, $12-15.

Comparison of flanged rim soup (left) and 7 5/8" soup plate (right).

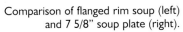

Small and large Lustre shell platters.

Lustre Shell covered sugar, $12-15; creamer, $8-10; demitasse cup and saucer, $15-18.

"Cup n' Saucer Candle" marketed as "Golden Lustre Glow Carnival Glass," with original box, $20-25.

Three Band cup and saucer, $3-4; Jane Ray demitasse cup and saucer, $20-25; Fish Scale cup and saucer, $12-15.

Lustre mugs from left: advertising mugs on D-handle and child's mug, $15-20 each. D-handle mug, $5-7.

Advertising mugs, $15-20.

60

Lustre pitchers. Two pitchers on left are from Mexico marked "Termo Crisa." Fire-King Lustre milk pitcher from breakfast set, $45-50. We have found several pieces which indicate they are from Mexico and Argentina in the Lancaster, Ohio, area. We have been unable to determine if Anchor Hocking manufactured these items for another company.

Lustre batter pitchers. Top: Colonial 1" band, $25-30. Bottom: 3/4" band, $25-30.

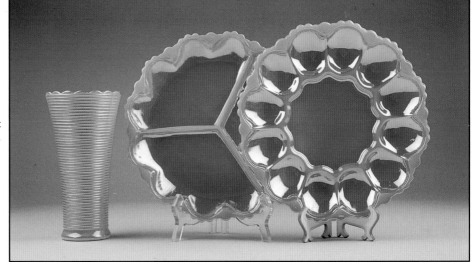

From left: Leaf plate, $8-10; Lotus bowl, $5-7; 7 1/2" bulb bowl/candy dish, $10-12; 6 3/4" ruffled diamond bowl, $12-15.

7" concentric ring vase, $18-20; three-part relish, $10-15; deviled egg tray, $15-20.

Back row: 5 1/4" Irish coffee mug, $8-10; D-handle mug, $5-7; breakfast bowl, $15-20; 4" x 4" leftover, $15-20. Front row: 4 3/8" tulip ashtray, $10-12; Shell candy dish, $15-18; 8" au gratin, $10-12; 4" ashtray, $8-10.

Lustre 3 3/8" vase, $10-12; 6 1/8" goblet, $10-15; 3" individual bean pot, $10-12; 3 3/4" flower pot, $12-15.

Lustre punch sets: Tom and Jerry with mugs, $50-60; Leaf set with punch cups, $40-50.

Colonial mixing bowls: 6", $15-18; 7 1/4", $15-20; 8 3/4", $20-25. Batter pitcher, $25-30.

Beaded-edge mixing bowls: 4 7/8", $10-12; 6", $15-18; 7 1/2", $15-18; 8 3/8", $22-25.

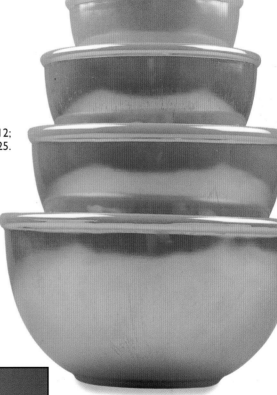

Swirl mixing bowls: 7", $15-20; 8", $15-20; 9", $20-25. Original box adds $10-15.

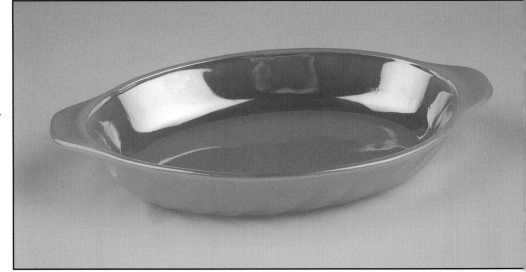

Advertisement for a large variety of Copper Tint ovenware. These items are relatively easy to find. Most items can be found in the $5-10 price range.

Lustre covered casserole, $15-20.

8" au gratin with swirl design, $10-12.

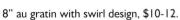

Rainbow / Fired-on Colors

Plain ball jugs. Small 42 oz. ball jugs: tangerine, $15-20; yellow, $50-60; cobalt, $75-85; green, $90-100. Large 80 oz. ball jugs: tangerine, $15-20; yellow, $75-85; cobalt, $90-100; green, $100-125.

Amazingly Low Priced!

New! Colorful!

"RAINBOW" LUNCHEON SET
No. 1700/60
26 PIECES » » 26 PIECES

. SANITARY
. . . EASY TO CLEAN
. . . . . . PERMANENT COLORS

Composition of set:
Four Cups
Four Saucers
Four 9½" Dinner Plates
Four 10 Oz. Footed Tumblers
Four Sherbets
Four Sherbet Plates
One Sugar
One Creamer

TANGERINE
BLUE
GREEN
YELLOW

Set can be had in assorted colors as illustrated above or will be packed only one color to a carton if desired.

ANCHOR HOCKING GLASS CORPORATION
HOCKING-DIVISION
LANCASTER, OHIO, U. S. A.

The variety of bold fired-on colors has made this glassware a favorite with collectors. Pitchers and tumblers are readily available; dinnerware is more difficult to locate. The condition of this glassware is of central importance to its value and collectability. The fired-on color chips off from regular use. This greatly reduces the value of the glassware.

We have had many requests for the fired-on red glassware pictured in a recent collector's book. This glassware is not red, but a bright orange. Sometimes photographs do not accurately portray their subject.

Many of these pieces are usually found in one of these colors and considerably rarer in other colors. Pitchers, for example, are most often found in orange; the smallest of the beaded mixing bowls is usually green, etc. Premium price are to be expected when these items are found in other colors.

Original Rainbow advertisement.

Cobalt blue dinnerware: 9 oz. tumbler, $10-12; 9" dinner, $10-12; 48 oz. ball jug, $75-85; 80 oz. ball jug, $90-100; 5" bowl (deep), $12-15; sugar, $8-10; creamer, $8-10; refrigerator dish with crystal cover, $15-18.

Tangerine pitchers and tumblers. 80 oz. ball jug, $15-20; Manhattan-style 42 oz. jugs, $30-35 (2 styles), 42 oz. plain jug, $15-20. 5 oz. juice tumbler, $8-10; 9 oz. tumbler, $10-12.

Tangerine dinnerware: 15 oz. footed tumbler, $12-15; sherbet, $8-10; 9" dinner plate, $10-12; 5" bowl, $12-15; cup and saucer, $8-10; sugar, $5-7; creamer, $5-7.

Tangerine ribbed shaker (not Anchor Hocking), $12-15 each; small bud vase, $8-10; small flower pot, $5-6.

Tangerine art deco vase, $12-15; ruffled flower pot, $10-12; scalloped planter, $10-12.

Refrigeratorware. Covered ribbed jug, $12-15; 5" x 10" leftover, $20-25; 5"x 5" leftover, $15-20; 5" round leftover, $15-18.

Pastel blue dinnerware. 9" dinner, $10-12; 7" salad plate, $8-10; cup/saucer, $8-10; creamer, $10-12; 6" bowl, $10-12; sherbet, $8-10; shaker, $12-15 each.

Pastel blue pitchers and tumbler. 80 oz. ball jug, $65-75; 42 oz. ball jug, $50-55; 9 oz. tumbler, $10-12; 5 oz. tumbler, $8-10.

Pastel blue art deco vase, $15-18; ruffled flower pot, $12-15; covered refrigerator jar, $20-25; planter, $12-15.

Yellow 42 oz. jug, $50-60; 9 oz. tumbler, $10-12; 80 oz. ball jug, $75-85.

Yellow dinnerware. Sugar, $10-12; 9" dinner plate, $10-12; 6" bowl, $10-12; 7" salad plate, $8-10; cup and saucer, $8-10; sherbet, $8-10.

Yellow dinnerware: 15 oz. footed tumbler, $12-15; cup, $5-7; deep bowl, $12-15; sherbet, $8-10.

Yellow Art Deco vase, $15-20; covered 5" round leftover, $18-20; 5"x5" leftover, $20-25.

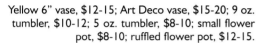

Yellow 6" vase, $12-15; Art Deco vase, $15-20; 9 oz. tumbler, $10-12; 5 oz. tumbler, $8-10; small flower pot, $8-10; ruffled flower pot, $12-15.

Pastel pitchers and tumblers. Blue 5 oz., $8-10; blue 9 oz., $10-12; pink 80 oz. ball jug, $50-60; blue 80 oz. ball jug, $65-75; blue 42 oz., $50-55; pink 42 oz., $45-50.

Pink 80 oz. pitcher, $50-60; pink 42 oz. Manhattan ball jug, $50-60; pink 42 oz. pitcher, $45-50; 9 oz. tumbler, $8-10.

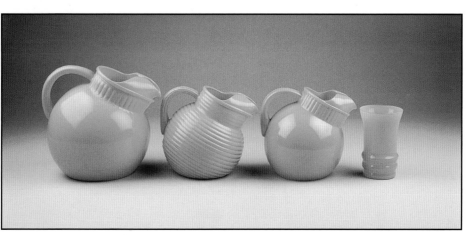

Pink dinnerware. Sugar, $10-12; creamer, $10-12; 9" dinner plate, $12-15; 7" salad plate, $10-12; cup and saucer, $8-10; 6" bowl, $12-15; sherbet, $8-10.

Pink 6" vase, $15-20; 5" round leftover, $20-25; hurricane lamp, $45-50.

Hazel Atlas fine ribbed 80 oz. jug, $100-125. Very similar to Fire-King jugs.

Dark green dinnerware: 9" dinner plate, $15-18; 7" salad plate, $12-15; 6" plate, $10-12; deep bowl, $20-25; sherbet, $12-15.

Light green (jadite color) dinnerware: creamer, $15-20; sugar, $15-20; 9" plate, $15-18; 7" plate, $12-15; 6" plate, $10-12; 6" bowl, $15-18; cup/saucer, $10-12; salt and pepper, $30-35 pr.

Dark green. 80 oz. ball jug, $100-125; 42 oz. jug, $90-100; 5" x 5" leftover, $30-35; 5" x 10" leftover, $40-45; 9 oz. tumbler, $18-20.

Wheat grease jar. Possibly after-factory, $45-50.

Chartreuse bowls: Large berry, $10-12; 6" cereal, $8-10; 4 1/2" small fruit, $5-6.

Brown and peach dinnerware. Brown: 10" plate, $12-15; 9" plate, $6-8; 7" plate, $5-7; saucer, $1-2; sugar, $8-10; creamer, $8-10. Peach: large berry, $10-12; 6" cereal, $8-10; cup, $3-4. Striped tumbler, $4-5.

Odd Shell cups. Fired-on blue, $12-15; green, $12-15.

Splash-proof two-quart mixing bowls. Green, $30-35; red, $25-30; yellow, $25-30.

Swirl mixing bowls, $75-100 set of four. Original decorated box, $15-20.

Brown 6" mixing bowl, $20-25.

Original box for beaded-edge mixing bowls, $20-25.

Beaded-edge mixing bowls, $75-85, set of four.

Spout-handled mixing bowls, $45-50 set.

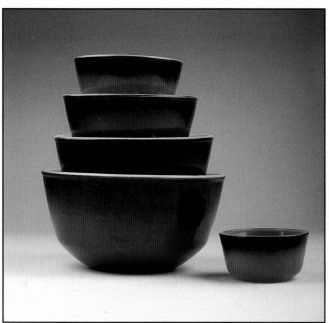

Brown mixing bowls, $40-45 set. Small brown bowl, $4-5.

Fired-on basketweave bowls, $12-15 each. Turquoise blue (not fired-on) basket weave bowl, $90-100.

Black-trimmed primary colors mixing bowl set, $50-60 set of four. Straight-sided dessert bowls, $8-10 each; mugs, $6-8 each.

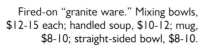

Fired-on "granite ware." Mixing bowls, $12-15 each; handled soup, $10-12; mug, $8-10; straight-sided bowl, $8-10.

Pastel leaf plates and blossom bowls, $12-15 each set.

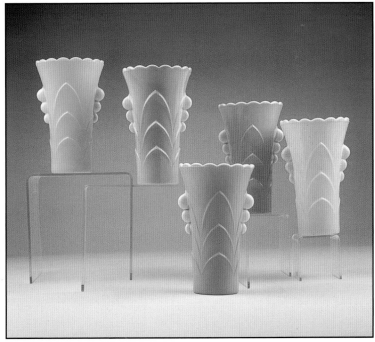

Leftovers. Bright red: 5" x 5", $20-25; 5" x 10", $30-35. Dark green: 5" x 5", $30-35; 5" x 10", $40-45. Yellow, 5" x 5", $20-25. White/Blue, 5" x 5", $20-25.

Vases. Yellow, 6", $10-12; flower pot, $12-15; Art Deco, $12-15; tangerine Art Deco, $12-15; green 6", $20-25.

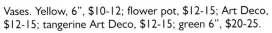

Art Deco vases with white handles, $12-15. each.

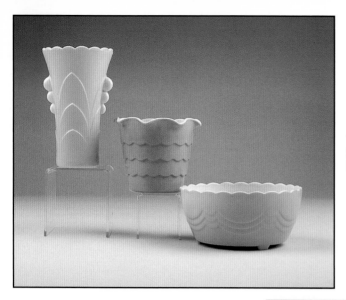

Yellow Art Deco vase (white interior), $12-15; blue/white ruffled flower pot, $10-12; green/white planter, $10-12.

Vitrock 7 1/2" vases. Red, $25-30; green, $18-20; white, $6-8; yellow, $12-15; cobalt, $20-25.

Swirl au gratin, $20-25.

Handled casseroles. Color fired-on by Color Craft, Indianapolis, Indiana, $5-10 each.

Handled casseroles, $5-10.

Handled soup mugs. Solid colors, $5-7; graniteware, $12-15; advertising, $6-8.

Fired-on bulb bowls. Yellow or green, $8-10; white, $5-7; red, $12-15; orange, $10-12.

Vitrock "Oyster and Pearl," green and peach. Handled 6" lemon bowl, $8-10; 10 3/4" console bowl, $15-20.

Vitrock "Oyster and Pearl"
console sets. Candles, $20-25
pair, console bowl, $15-20.

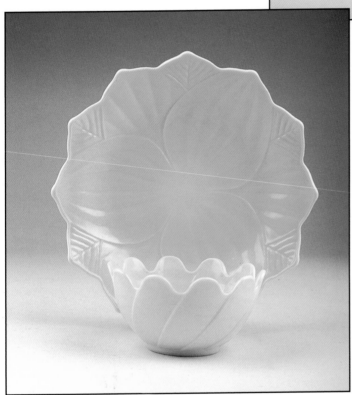

Vitrock leaf plate, $6-8; blossom
bowl, $5-7.

Square roll top cigarette/jewel
boxes, $15-18; round powder
boxes, $15-20.

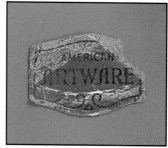

Shallow flower tray/bowl, $12-15 each; Waterford ashtray, $6-8.

Close-up of "Artware" label.

Bubble bowls, $12-15; lace-edge sherbet, $6-8.

Ruffled, diamond bottom bowls, $10-12 each; ruffled flower pot, $10-12.

White Dinnerware

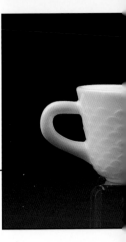

White dinnerware, especially Restaurantware, is an affordable substitute or complement to Fire-King's colored glassware. Since it was made for institutions, large sets can be found of this durable glassware.

Fishscale, especially the trimmed red and blue, is difficult to find today. Listed as Vitrock, a term given to many of Anchor Hocking's solid white patterns, "Fish Scale" is the name appropriately given by collectors.

Fishscale Vitrock dinnerware. 9 1/4" dinner, $10-12; 7 3/8" salad plate, $6-8; 8 3/4" vegetable, $20-22; 7 1/2" soup, $12-15; cup/saucer, $5-7.

Bubble white dinnerware. Clockwise from left: 7 3/4" flatsoup, $8-10; 8 3/8" large berry bowl, $6-8; deep cereal (scarce), $20-25; 9 1/2" dinner, $5-7; cup/saucer, $3-4; 4 1/2" fruit, $5-7; 5 1/4" cereal, $6-8; creamer, $5-6; sugar, $5-6.

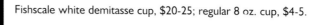
Fishscale white demitasse cup, $20-25; regular 8 oz. cup, $4-5.

Fishscale with blue trim. Dinner plate, $20-25; salad plate, $18-20; 5 1/2" deep cereal, $20-25; cup/saucer, $18-20.

Fishscale with red trim. Dinner plate, $18-20; 8 3/4" vegetable, $22-25; 5 1/2" deep cereal, $18-20; 5 1/2" dessert bowl, $10-12; cup/saucer, $12-15; 7 1/2" soup plate, $20-25.

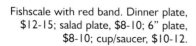
Fishscale with red band. Dinner plate, $12-15; salad plate, $8-10; 6" plate, $8-10; cup/saucer, $10-12.

Jane-Ray Vitrock dinnerware. Large berry, $18-20; dinner plate, $10-12; fruit bowl, $6-8; deep cereal, $12-15; cup/saucer, $6-8; ribbed bowl with cover, $15-18.

Milk White 4000 line dinnerware. Creamer, $5-6; sugar, $5-6; dinner plate, $8-10; salad plate, $8-10; 6" plate (scarce), $8-10; 8" vegetable, $15-18; 6 1/2" soup, $15-18; cup/saucer, $5-7. Holder for 3 sizes of plates, $20-25.

Sugar bowl, $5-6; sugar cover, $12-15; creamer, $5-6.

Milk White 1700 line. Dinner plate, $5-6; St. Denis cup/saucer (left), $6-8; Ransom cup/saucer (right), $8-10.

Close-up of Milk White label.

Laurel White. 9" dinner plate, $12-15; sugar, $8-10; cup, $5-7.

Restaurantware. 4 3/4" fruit, $5-7; 15 oz. bowl, $12-15; 11 1/2" oval platter, $18-20; mug/cup, $6-8; 9 1/2" oval platter, $18-20; heavy mug, $12-15; 9" dinner plate, $12-15; cup/saucer, $8-10; flanged rim cereal/grapefruit, $12-15; 10 oz. bowl, $12-15; 6 3/4" pie plate, $5-7; 3-part grill plate, $12-15; 5 1/2" bread and butter plate, $4-5.

Royal White dinnerware. 13" platter, $20-25; dinner plate, $8-10; 9" lunch plate, $10-12; 7" salad plate, $5-7; cup/saucer, $4-5; demitasse cup/saucer, $18-20; 4 3/4" dessert, $3-4; flat soup, $18-20.

Royal White 8 1/2" vegetable, $18-20; flat soup, $18-20.

Golden Shell dinnerware. 15" platter, $8-10; 10" dinner plate, $4-5; 9" lunch plate (rare), $18-20; 7 1/4" salad plate, $3-4; covered sugar, $8-10; creamer, $4-6; rim soup, $18-20; 4 3/4" dessert, $3-4; 7 5/8" flat soup, $8-10; 6 1/2" cereal, $6-8; 8 1/2" round vegetable, $10-12; demitasse cup/saucer, $8-10; cup/saucer, $3-4.

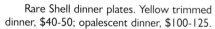

Original box for Golden Shell luncheon set. Box, $15-20.

Rare Shell dinner plates. Yellow trimmed dinner, $40-50; opalescent dinner, $100-125.

Aurora Shell, (mother-of-pearl finish). Clockwise from left: 8 1/2" round vegetable, $25-30; 7" plate, $10-12; flanged rim soup, $40-45; covered sugar, $30-35; creamer, $15-20; 4 3/4" fruit, $12-15; 6 3/8" cereal, $15-18; 7 5/8" soup plate, $20-22; demitasse cup/saucer, $35-40; regular cup/saucer, $20-25.

Shell flanged soup, $35-40.

Golden Anniversary: gold trimmed white Swirl dinnerware. 8 1/4" vegetable, $8-10; 12" platter, $8-10; 9" dinner, $3-4; 7" salad plate, $3-4; creamer, $4-5; sugar, $4-5; cup/saucer, $3-4; 4 7/8" dessert bowl, $3-4; 7 5/8" flat soup, $6-8.

Patio Pack. Oval plate, $6-8; handled mug, $5-7. Original box, $8-10.

Trimmed dinnerware. Sugar, $6-8; creamer, $6-8; 12" platter, $12-15; mixing bowl set, $40-45; 5" dessert bowl, $4-6.

Multi-color striped cup/saucer, $8-10.

Vitrock dinnerware with floral band. 10" dinner plate, $8-10; 8 5/8" lunch, $4-6; 7" salad, $4-6; creamer, $6-8; sugar, $6-8; cup/saucer, $4-5; 5" dessert bowl, $5-6; 6" cereal, $8-10; 9" large vegetable, $12-15.

White Dinnerware with Decals and Decorations

This section includes some of the most sought after of Fire-King patterns. Game Birds, Anniversary Rose, and Primrose are among the most passionately collected Fireking patterned dinnerware. These patterns contain enough commonly found pieces so one can easily put together a set and a few rare pieces to keep the collecting game interesting. The decorated Lace Edge plates and comports that match some of these patterns are most avidly sought.

Anniversary Rose dinner and kitchenware. 12" platter, $18-20; 10" dinner plate, $10-12; 7" salad plate, $12-15; covered sugar, $15-20; creamer, $8-10; cup/saucer, $5-7; 4 5/8" berry, $8-10; 6 1/2" soup, $15-20; 8 1/4" large vegetable, $20-25.

Anniversary Rose snack set. 11" x 6" plate with cup ring, $5-6; 5 oz. cup, $3-4; 5" chili bowl, $15-18; D-handled mug, $20-25.

Catalog ad for Anniversary Rose.

Anniversary Rose mixing bowls. One-quart, $50-60; 1-1/2 quart, $40-45; 2-1/2 quart, $40-45; 3-1/2 quart, $50-60.

Two styles of Anniversary Rose mixing bowls.

BBQ Chef. These pieces were made by Anchor Hocking and Hazel Atlas. Ashtray, $15-20; salt/pepper, $18-20; Hazel Atlas mug, $8-10; Fire-King dinner plate, $20-25.

Blue Mosaic dinnerware. 8 1/4" vegetable, $15-20; 12" platter, $12-15; 10" dinner, $8-10; 7" salad plate, $6-8; covered sugar, $8-10; creamer, $5-7; cup/saucer, $4-5; 4 5/8" dessert, $4-6; 6 1/2" soup, $12-15.

Blue Mosaic lunch set. Box adds $8-10.

Blue Mosaic label.

Fleurette dinnerware. 8 1/4" vegetable, $10-12; 12" platter, $12-15; 9 1/8" dinner, $4-5; 7 3/8" salad plate, $8-10; 6" plate, $15-20; covered sugar, $8-10; creamer, $5-7; snack plate, $4-5; snack cup, $2-3; 4 5/8" dessert, $4-5; 6 5/8" soup, $8-10; cup/saucer, $4-5; mug (scarce), $45-50.

Fleurette 13" lace-edge plate, $100-150.

Forget-Me-Not dinnerware. 12" platter, $15-18; 10" dinner, $8-10; covered sugar, $8-10; creamer, $6-8; cup/saucer, $8-10; 4 5/8" dessert, $6-8; 6 5/8" soup, $12-15; 8 1/4" vegetable, $15-18.

Forget-Me-Not mug, $20-25.

Forget-Me-Not ovenware. Oval casserole, $20-25; mug, $20-25; custard, $10-12; chili bowl, $15-18; loaf pan, $20-25.

Game birds, Ruffled Grouse. Dinner plate, $8-10; 6" plate, $10-12; 11 oz. tumbler, $12-15; juice tumbler, $25-30; 8 oz. mug, $10-12; ashtray, $12-15; 4 5/8" dessert, $6-8; chili bowl, $8-10.

Game birds, Canadian Goose. Dinner plate, $8-10; 6" plate, $10-12; mug, $10-12; ashtray, $12-15; 4 5/8" dessert, $6-8; chili bowl, $8-10; juice tumbler, $25-30; 11 oz. tumbler, $12-15.

Game birds, Ringed-neck Pheasant. 12" platter, $35-45; dinner, $8-10; 6" plate; $10-12; 11 oz. tumbler, $12-15; juice tumbler, $25-30; mug, $10-12; ashtray, $12-15; 4 5/8" dessert, $6-8; chili bowl, $8-10; 8 1/4" vegetable, $40-50; covered sugar, $25-30; creamer, $20-25.

91

Game birds, Mallard Duck. Dinner plate, $8-10; 6" plate, $10-12; 11 oz. tumbler, $12-15; juice tumbler, $25-30; mug, $10-12; ashtray, $12-15; 4 5/8" dessert, $6-8; chili bowl, $8-10.

Mallard Duck ashtray, $12-15.

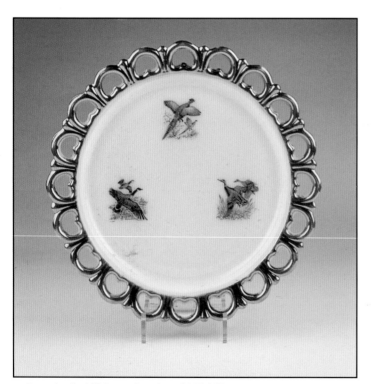

Game birds. 13" lace-edge plate, $150-200.

Turkey cup, $75-100.

Harvest dinnerware. 8 1/4" vegetable, $10-12; 12" platter, $10-12; 10" dinner, $5-7; 7 3/8" salad plate, $5-7; covered sugar, $8-10; creamer, $5-7; cup/saucer, $4-5; 4 5/8" dessert, $4-5; covered butter (no pattern), $35-40; gravy (no pattern), $15-20; 6 5/8" soup, $6-8.

Homestead dinnerware. 12" platter, $12-15; 10" dinner, $5-7; 7 3/8" salad plate, $8-10; creamer, $4-5; covered sugar, $6-8; cup/saucer, $4-5; 4 5/8" dessert, $4-5; 6 5/8" soup, $10-12; 8 1/4" vegetable, $12-15. Black-ringed range shakers, $18-20 pr.

Honey Suckle dinnerware. 12" platter, $12-15; 9 1/8" dinner, $5-7; 7 3/8" salad plate, $4-6; 6" plate, $10-15; covered sugar, $8-10; creamer, $5-7; cup/saucer, $4-5; 4 5/8" dessert, $4-5; 6 5/8" soup, $10-12 (two styles); 8 1/4" vegetable, $12-15. Juice tumbler, $12-15; 9 oz. water, $10-12; 12 oz. iced tea, $12-15. Go-along red range shakers, $18-20 pr.

Honey Suckle box, $10-15.

Close-up of two styles of Honey Suckle soups.

Lace-edge 8 1/4" salad plates. Hand-painted birds, $20-25; floral, $15-20.

Lace-edge 11" hand-painted floral
bowl, $35-40; 11" gold decals, $25-30;
7" covered comport, golf trim, $15-20.

Fleurette 13" chop plate, $100-150.

Lace-edge 13" cake plates. Floral, $25-30; Couple on a couch, $20-25.

Hand-painted floral console set. Candles, $25-30 pr., 11" bowl, $35-40.

Holiday lace-edge. 8 1/4" plates, $20-25; sherbets, $15-20.

Primrose 11" bowl, $150-175.

Lake Como. Salt and pepper, $50-60 pr.; 9" vegetable, $50-60; cup/saucer, $30-35.

Lake Como. Brown dinner, $40-50; shakers, $50-60; cereal, $25-30; cup/saucer, $30-35.

Meadow Green dinnerware. 12" platter, $6-8; 10" dinner, $3-4; 7 3/8" salad plate, $2-3; cup/saucer, $2-3; 4 5/8" dessert, $2-3; 6 5/8" soup, $4-6; 8 1/4" vegetable, $8-10.

Meadow Green ovenware. Covered casseroles, $8-10 each. 5" x 9" loaf pan, $6-8; two-quart utility, $8-10; mixing bowls, $6-8 each.

Meadow Green kitchenware. Mixing bowls: 1 1/2-quart, $8-10; two-quart, $8-10; 2 1/2-quart, $10-12; mug, $4-5; cereal bowl, $4-5; French casserole, $8-10; custard, $2-3.

Meadow Green catalog ad.

Meadow Green Fire-King Ovenware

photo ref.	description	item order no.	dozen	lbs.	price doz.
A		WH433/75			
B		W434/75			
C		W338/75			
D		WH436/75			
E		WH437/75			
F		WH438/75			
G		WH439/75			

NOTE: See index for additional listings of Meadow Green bulk and gift items.

Meadow Green boxed casserole set.

ANCHOR HOCKING
Meadow Green
6-piece Casserole Set

16 Piece
DINNERWARE SET
Meadow Green Pattern
W4600/SS

Original box for Meadow Green dinnerware.

Peach Blossom dinnerware, hand-painted. This painting is different from that on the ovenware that was produced by Gay Fad. 9 1/8" dinner, $18-20; 7 3/8" salad plate, $12-15; 8 3/8" vegetable (Bubble), $25-30; tumbler, $10-12; 4 7/8" dessert, $12-15; cup/saucer, $25-30; salt/pepper, $20-25 pr.

Gay Fad Peach Blossom. Loaf pan, 5" x 9", $15-18; 8"x 12" utility, $20-25; 8"square cake, $18-20.

Gay Fad Peach Blossom. Casseroles. One-quart, $20-25; one pint, $20-25; au gratin, $25-30.

Gay Fad Peach Blossom kitchenware. Handled French casserole with cover, $15-18; mug, $10-12; chili bowl, $8-10; custard, $3-4.

Gay Fad Peach Blossom refrigerator jars. 4"
round, $15-18; 4" x 9" oval, $20-25; 4" square,
$8-10; 4"x 8", $15-18.

Primrose dinnerware. 12" platter, $12-15; 10" dinner plate,
$8-10; 7 3/8" salad plate, $5-7; covered sugar, $8-10;
creamer, $5-7; cup/saucer, $4-5; 4 5/8" dessert, $4-5; 6 5/8"
soup, $8-10; 8 1/4" vegetable, $12-15. Juice tumbler, $20-
25; crystal water tumbler, $35-40; 11 oz. tumbler, $18-20.

Primrose snack set. Plate, $5-7; cup,
$3-4. Original boxes, $5-10.

Primrose three-part relish, $100-125;
salt and pepper shaker, $175-200 pair.

Primrose 11" footed comports (two styles), $150-175.

Vienna Lace one-quart casserole (scarce), $30-40.

Primrose ovenware. One-quart casserole, $12-15; 1 1/2-quart casserole, $12-15; one-pint casserole, $12-15; custard, $4-5; loaf pan with cover, $15-18; utility pan, 6" x 10", $10-12; 8" x 10", $20-25; 8" cake pan, $12-15.

Vienna Lace dinnerware. Some pieces do not have center design. 12" platter (two styles), $12-15; 10" dinner, $8-10; covered sugar, $6-8; creamer, $5-7; go-along demi saucer, $6-8; 4 5/8" dessert, $4-6; 6 5/8" soup, $8-10; 8 1/4" vegetable, $12-15. 7 5/8" plate (no design), $3-4; handled soup (no design) $4-5; cup/saucer (no design), $4-5.

Wheat dinnerware. 11 oz. crystal tumbler, $8-10; 12"
platter, $12-15; 10" dinner, $5-7; 7 5/8" salad plate,
$6-8; covered sugar, $8-10; creamer, $5-7; 5 oz. juice
tumbler, $6-8; cup/saucer, $4-5; custard, $2-3; 4 5/8"
dessert, $3-4; 6 5/8" soup, $6-8; 8 oz. mug, $35-40; 8
1/4" vegetable, $10-12.

Wheat 8 oz. mug with original label, $35-40.

Wheat boxed sets. Snack plate, $2-3;
snack cup, $1-2.

Wheat ovenware. One-quart casserole,
$8-10; 8" x 12" utility pan, $12-15;
square cake, $10-12; custard, $2-3;
covered loaf pan, $12-15.

Wheat label.

Wheat ovenware. One-quart casserole, $8-10; 1 1/2-quart au gratin, $12-15; one-pint casserole, $10-12; 5" handled baking dish, $15-18; 8" x 12" utility, $12-15; round cake, $10-12.

Wheat pie baker with variant decal, $20-25.

Wheat catalog ad.

Mugs and Bowls

Decorated mugs and bowls, for the most part, are readily available today. But there are so many items to collect and some rarities that collectors can hunt for years. These items were produced for over 30 years. The best way to determine age is by the subject matter.

Exxon items. Clear tumbler, $4-6; pitcher, $15-20; frosted tumblers, $5-7; coffee mugs, $3-4. Go-along metal tray, $10-12.

Yellowstone Park souvenir Bubble cereal bowl, $12-15.

Yellowstone Park souvenir Bubble bowl with bears, $12-15.

Advertising mugs, $5-10 each.

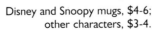

Zodiac mugs, $3-4.

Disney and Snoopy mugs, $4-6;
other characters, $3-4.

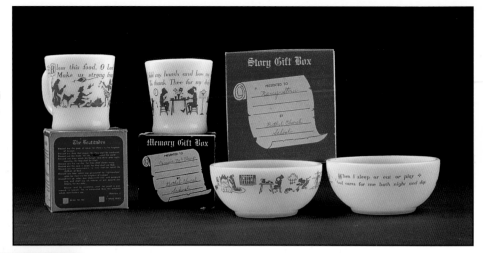

Nursery Rhyme mugs, $6-8; chili bowls, $5-7.

Davy Crockett breakfast bowls, $25-30; mugs, $12-15.

Davy Crockett bowls, $20-25.

Davy Crockett Hunter or Statesman bowl, $30-35. Tumbler, $18-20.

Batman chili bowl, $20-25; Batman mug, $10-15.

Canadian Club Gamebirds ashtray, $20-25.

Tulip cottage cheese bowls, $5-7; with cover, $10-12.

Flamingo relish dish, $50-60.

Children's Days of the Week bowls, $6-8.

Hand-painted Floral plates, $20-25 each.

Hand-painted Scene plates, $25-30 each.

Bird plates, $20-25 each.

107

Scene plates, $25-30 each.

Comic plates, $20-25 each.

Scene plates, $25-30; rose plate, $15-20.

Decal platter, $15-20; Jesus decal, $10-15; hand-painted covered bridge platter, $30-35.

Lace-edge covered bridge, $25-30 each; barn plate, $20-25.

Holly decal on Swirl cup/saucer, $25-30 set.

Maw and Paw plates, $10-12 each; Mama mug, $8-10.

Pointer plate, $30-35.

Souvenir scenic plate (very colorful), $30-35.

Institutional Dinnerware

We have termed these late Fire-King patterns (ca. 1960-76) "institutional ware" because they were heavily marketed to diners, restaurants, and cafeterias, however company catalogues clearly indicate that they were sold for home use as well. Only the advertising items are currently in demand. This dinnerware is fun and affordable.

Athena dinnerware.

Institutional dinnerware from L & K restaurants.

Waffle House platter, $10-15.

Springwood dinnerware.

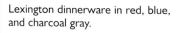

Institutional dinnerware from Allentown, Pennsylvania.

Lexington dinnerware in red, blue, and charcoal gray.

111

Decorated Kitchenware

This section includes decorated Fire-King kitchenware lines that do not include dinnerware – no plates, cups, or small bowls. Rather, these items were for use in the kitchen and oven. Some of these items were give-a-ways or very reasonably priced promotional items.

The mixing bowl sets are extremely popular, even with people who have never heard of Fire-King. The splash-proof bowls with tulip, apple, and kitchen utensils decorating the side are ideal both for use and display. The Kitchen Aids bowls with blue and yellow decals are extremely rare. The Spag's Kitchen Aids bowl only comes in one size and was a promotional item for Spag's stores.

Blue and Gold Feather ovenware and kitchenware. 8 3/8" mixing bowl, $15-18; 7 1/4" mixing bowl, $12-15; 1 1/2-quart casserole, $18-20; 4" x 8" leftover, $20-25; batter pitcher, $25-30; 8" square cake, $12-15; 8" round cake, $12-15; 4"x 4" leftover, $12-15; 8" x 12" baking pan, $15-18; loaf pan, $12-15.

Blue Heaven kitchenware. Large mixing bowl, $18-20; medium mixing bowl, $15-18; small mixing bowl, $15-18; mug, $5-7; custard, $3-4; French casserole, $10-12. Large tumbler, $8-10; small tumbler, $5-7.

Blue Heaven ovenware. 1 1/2-quart casserole, $15-20; 8" square cake, $10-12; loaf pan, $10-12; 8" round cake, $10-12.

Candleglow kitchenware. Three-quart casserole, $12-15; two-quart, $10-12; 1 1/2-quart, $10-12; mug, $4-6; custard, $2-3; cereal bowl, $5-6.

Candleglow mixing bowl set, $35-40 set; with box, $40-45.

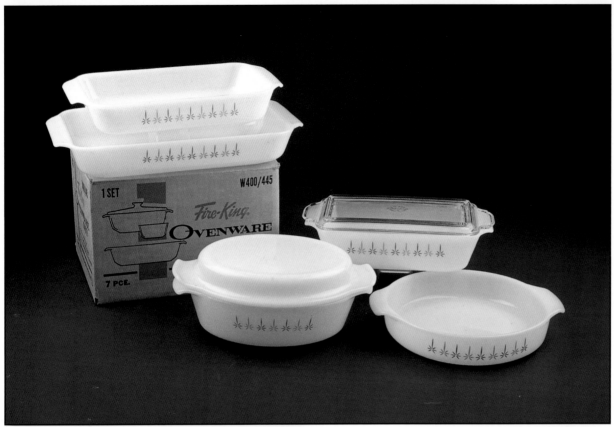

Candleglow ovenware. Large utility pan, $8-10; small utility pan, $6 8; loaf pan, $8-10; round cake, $6-8; covered au gratin, $15-18.

Candleglow label.

Candleglow label.

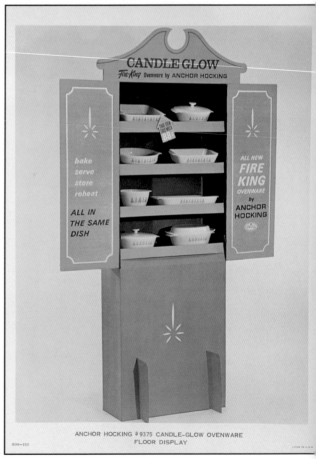

Candleglow store display.

Chanticleer ovenware. Oval au gratin, $18-20; two-quart casserole, $12-15; one-pint casserole, $12-15; 1 1/2-quart casserole, $12-15.

Chanticleer ovenware. 8" Square cake, $8-10; 8" x 12" utility pan, $10-12; 8" round cake, $8-10; loaf pan, $10-12.

Chanticleer mixing bowl set, $40-50.

Chanticleer kitchenware. French casserole, $10-12; mug, $20-25; chili bowl, $10-12; custard, $3-4; snack cup, $15-20.

Currier and Ives kitchenware. Custard, $3-5; large mixing bowl, $15-20; medium mixing bowl, $12-15; small mixing bowl, $12-15; mug, $10-12; chili bowl, $8-10; French casserole, $12-15.

Currier and Ives ovenware. 6" x 10" utility pan, $12-15; 8" cake, $10-12; loaf pan, $10-12.

Mushroom kitchenware and ovenware. Mixing bowl set, $40-50; covered au gratin, $20-22.

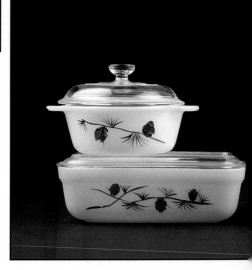

Pinecone. One-pint casserole, $18-20; oil and vinegar, $18-20 pr.; salt and pepper, $8-10 set; custard, $4-5; 4"x 8" leftover, $22-25.

Nature's Bounty. Two-quart casserole, $10-12; au gratin, $12-15; one-quart casserole, $12-15; 1 1/2 quart casserole, $10-12.

Catalog ad for Nature's Bounty.

Nature's Bounty. Mixing bowl set of 4, $30-40; mug, $8-10; custard, $3-4.

Summerfield mixing bowl set, $30-40; custard, $4-5.

Summerfield. Large utility pan, $10-12; loaf pan, $8-10; small utility pan, $8-10; 8" square cake, $10-12; 8" round cake, $8-10.

Summerfield ovenware. Oval au gratin, $18-20; loaf pan, $8-10; one-quart casserole, $12-15; small utility pan, $8-10; large utility pan, $10-12.

Summerfield catalog ad.

Fire-King ovenware. Pattern unknown. One-quart casserole, $10-12; au gratin, $15-18; loaf pan, $8-10; utility pan, $10-12. Go-along shakers, $15-20 pr.

Le Bon Potager ovenware. Au gratin, $20-22; loaf pan, $12-15; French casserole, $8-10; individual casserole, $12-15; 1 1/2-quart casserole, $12-15.

Mixing bowl set, $20-25 set.

Castleware. Two-quart casserole, $10-12; au gratin, $12-15; French casserole, $6-8; 1 1/2-quart casserole, $8-10; loaf pan, $6-8; individual casserole, $6-8; mixing bowl, $8-10.

Leftovers. 4" x 4" floral, $10-12; 4" x 8" floral, $18-20; 4" x 4" feather, $8-10.

Apples (Apples and Cherries) kitchenware. Mixing bowls: one-quart, $40-45; two-quart, $35-40; three-quart, $40-45; four-quart, $45-50. Grease jar, $45-50; shakers, $65-75 pr.

Colonial Kitchen with diamonds. Mixing bowls: 6", $45-50; 7 1/4", $50-55; 8 3/4", $55-60. Batter bowl with red trim, $50-60.

Original advertisement for Diamond set.

White Colonial Kitchen. Batter pitcher, $20-25; 6" mixing bowl, $15-20; 7 1/4", $15-20; 8 3/4", $15-20.

Colonial kitchen 7 1/4" bowl with green band. Unusual, $75-100.

Colonial Kitchen with solid bands. Mixing bowls: 6", $25-30; 7 1/4", $30-35; 8 3/4", $35-40; shakers, $45-50 pair; covered grease jar, $30-35.

Four-piece set with original box, $160-180.

Black Dots. Mixing bowls: one-quart, $30-35; two-quart, $30-35; three-quart, $35-40; four-quart, $40-45; shakers, $50-60 pr., grease jar, $40-45.

Red Dots. Mixing bowls, one-quart, $30-35; two-quart, $30-35; three-quart, $35-40; four-quart, $40-45; shakers, $50-60; grease jar, $40-45.

Kitchen Aids kitchenware. Mixing bowls: one-quart, $100-125; two-quart, $75-85; three-quart, $100-125; four-quart, $100-125; shakers, $140-160 pr., grease jar, $90-100.

Kitchen Aids mixing bowls. Four-quart red, $100-125; three-quart yellow, $350-400; two-quart blue, $350-400; one-quart red, $100-125

Rare Kitchen Aids mixing bowls.

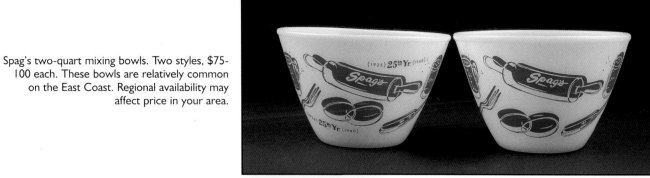

Spag's two-quart mixing bowls. Two styles, $75-100 each. These bowls are relatively common on the East Coast. Regional availability may affect price in your area.

Modern Tulip. Grease jar, $25-30; shakers, $35-45 pair; one-quart, $25-30; two-quart, $20-25; three-quart, $20-25; four-quart, $25-30.

Modern Tulip grease jars in black (left) and cobalt (right). Items with cobalt are very scarce. At least 2 to 3 times value of black.

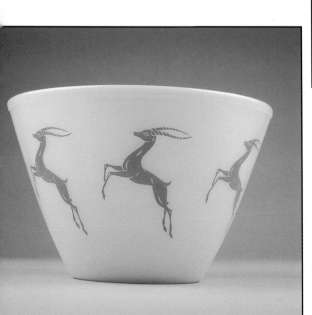

Leaping Stag bowl. Only found in four-quart size, $20-25.

Original box for Swirl mixing bowls, $5-10.

Swirl mixing bowls: 5", $20-25; 6", $10-15; 7", $10-15; 8", $10-15; 9", $10-15. Swirl casserole, $10-15.

Tulips on ivory. Grease jar, $40-50; shakers, $50-60; one-quart, $35-40; two-quart, $35-40; three-quart, $35-40; four-quart, $40-45.

Original box for range set, $10-15.

Tulips on white. Mixing bowls: one-quart, $40-45; two-quart, $40-45; three-quart, $40-45; four-quart, $45-50; grease jar, $50-55; shakers, $75-85.

White mixing bowl sets. Splash-proof (4 bowls), $80-100 set; Swirl (5 bowls), $70-80; Colonial Kitchen (3 bowls), $45-50; beaded-edge (4 bowls), $50-60; straight-sided (4 bowls), $40-50.

Straight-sided white mixing bowls, $10-15 each; jadite (rare), $500+.

Gay Fad

Gay Fad Studios purchased items from a variety of local companies to decorate in their Lancaster, Ohio, studio. Located just across the street, they used Anchor Hocking as one of their suppliers, but their designs can be found on glass of many other companies, especially Hazel Atlas.

Gay Fad's Gaytime Accessories are hand-painted items found in a variety of patterns. Individual pieces will vary, especially those with Poinsettias and Apples on them. Distlefink is the most highly sought after of these patterns and the most expensive.

The Gay Fad Story. Original Brochure.

Distlefink mixing bowls: four-quart, $125-150; three-quart blue, $200-225; three-quart red (not pictured), $125-150; two-quart, $125-150; one-quart, $150-175.

Distlefink Colonial Kitchen 8 3/4" bowl, $200-250.

Distlefink casseroles. Clockwise from left: 6" x 10" baker, $100-125; 1 1/2-quart (red), $100-125; loaf pan, $90-100; one-pint, $90-100; oval au gratin, $125-150; blue 1 1/2-quart, $125-150.

Distlefink lace-edge 8" plate, $45-50; 4" x 8" leftover, $100-125.

Gay Fad Apple mixing bowls: 7", $45-50; 8", $45-50; 9", $45-50.

Gay Fad Apple. 9" pie plate, $30-35; 10" round cake pan, $40-45; 11" rectangular utility pan, $40-45; 9 1/2" loaf pan, $40-45.

Gay Fad Apple. 1 1/2-quart covered casserole with holder, $65-75; custards, $10-12; individual pie, $20-25; one-quart casserole, $50-60.

Gay Fad Poppy. Clockwise from top left: loaf pan, $35-40; 11" utility pan, $35-40; custards, $10-12; 10" round cake, $35-40.

Gay Fad Poppy casseroles. two-quart, $50-50; one-quart, $45-50; 1 1/2-quart, $50-55.

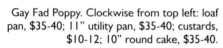

Gay Fad Poppy frosted glassware. Batter pitcher, $30-35; syrup, $25-30; tumblers, $10-12.

Gay Fad Poinsettia. 10" round cake, $40-45; 9" pie plate, $30-35; yellow individual pie, $45-50; comport, $75-100; custard, $10-12; 6" swirl bowl, $40-45; loaf pan, $40-50.

Poinsettia comport, $75-100.

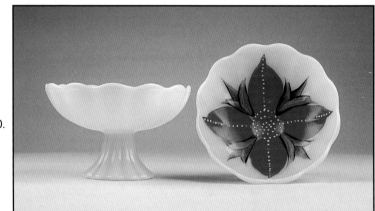

Swirl mixing bowls. Poinsettia 6", $40-45; Apple 7", $45-50; Apple 8", $45-50.

Poinsettia 10" round cake, $40-45; Apple loaf pan, $40-45; Poppy one-quart casserole, $45-50.

Outlined Fruit. 1 1/2-quart casserole, $30-35. Splash Proof mixing bowls: one-quart, $90-100; two-quart, $60-70; three-quart, $60-70; four-quart, $65-75; one-pint casserole, $35-40.

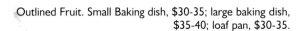

Outlined Fruit. Small Baking dish, $30-35; large baking dish, $35-40; loaf pan, $30-35.

Fruit kitchenware. Mixing bowls, tab handled: one-quart, $30-35; 1 1/2-quart, $30-35; 2 1/2-quart, $40-45. French casserole, $10-15; stacking mug, $10-12; two-quart casserole, $25-30; custard, $6-8; 5" bowl, $8-10.

Fruit Colonial Kitchenware mixing bowls: 6", $20-25; 7 1/4", $25-30; 8 3/4", $25-30; batter pitcher, $150-175.

Fruit. 1 1/2-quart au gratin, $25-30; covered loaf pan, $30-35; 6" x 10" baking dish, $25-30; 8" square cake, $25-30.

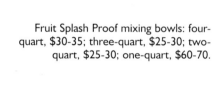

Fruit Splash Proof mixing bowls: four-quart, $30-35; three-quart, $25-30; two-quart, $25-30; one-quart, $60-70.

Fruit. Splash Proof four-quart mixing bowl, $30-35; 11" divided casserole, $25-30; 1 1/2-quart covered casserole, $30-35; French casserole, $10-15; cup/saucer, $10-12; 1 1/2-quart au gratin, $30-35.

Fruit. 4" x 4" leftover, $10-15; 4" x 8" leftover, $20-25; 8" oval leftover, $20-25; chili bowl, $8-10; large custard, $15-20; mug, $10-12; small custard, $4-5; covered sugar, $10-15; creamer, $10-15.

Fruit casseroles. 1 1/2-quart, $30-35; one-quart, $25-30; one-pint, $30-35; two-quart decorated cover, $30-35..

French casseroles, $10-15. Banana (scarce), $65-75.

Fruit cups and saucers, $10-12.

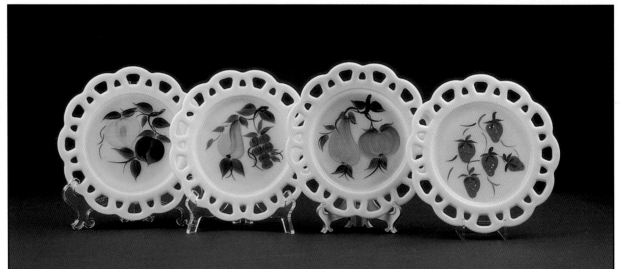

8" lace-edge Fruit plates, $15-20 each.

Large custard, $15-20

Satin Fruit salad set. Large salad bowl, $20-25; small bowls, $5-8; cruet, $10-12; salt and pepper, $10-15 set.

Satin Fruit pitcher and tumblers. Pitcher, $20-25; tumblers, $8-10.

Fruit Apple ball jug, $75-100; tumbler, $10-12; cruet, $15-18.

Fruit pitcher, $18-20; tumblers, $8-10; shakers, $12-15 pr.

Yellow Rose. 4" x 4" leftover, $25-30; 4" x 8", $40-45; two-quart mixing bowl, $45-50.

134

Sapphire Blue

Sapphire Blue Oven Glass is among the most recognized of Anchor Hocking's products. Produced for nearly 20 years, this sturdy glass is pale blue with the decorative Philbe design. It was originally produced in 1940 as a dinnerware line in Depression Glass colors. A very limited amount of this line was produced. It was transformed into Sapphire Blue Oven Ware and became very popular.

Casserole dishes, custards, and pie plates are the most frequently seen pieces in this line. Others like the skillet and the baby bottle covers are extremely rare. Some pieces are found without the Philbe design.

Also included in this section are other patterns that Anchor Hocking produced in this light blue color.

Sapphire Blue casseroles and roasters. Pie plate lid casseroles: two-quart, $20-25; 1 1/2-quart, $20-22; one-quart, $20-22. Roasters: 10 1/2", $75-85; 8 3/4", $45-50.

Knob handle lid casseroles: two-quart, $20-25; 1 1/2-quart (not pictured), $20-25; one-quart, $20-22; one-pint, $18-20; individual, $10-12. Table server (base for casserole), $18-20.

Sapphire Blue leftovers and baking pans. 4 1/2" x 5" leftover, $10-12; 5" x 9", $25-30; 8" x 10 1/2" utility, $20-22; loaf pan, $20-25.

Sapphire Blue mixing/utility bowls: 6 7/8", $20-22; 8 3/8", $22-25; 10 1/8", $25-30.

10 1/2" roaster, $75-85; with box add $5-10.

Original box, $5-10.

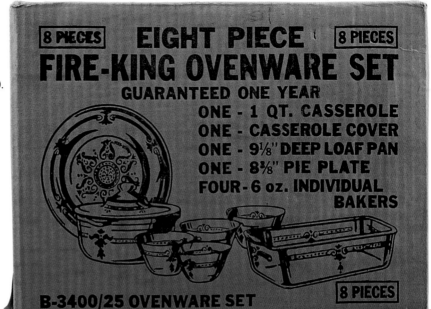

Layer cake pan, 9", $30-35.

Pie plates: 9 1/2", $10-12; 8 1/4", $10-12. Juice saver, $150-175.

Utility pan, 8" x 12", $75-85.

Sapphire Blue skillet, 7"
plus handle, $400-450.

Sapphire Blue custards/jelly jars. 2 1/8" no design jelly jar, $8-10; 2 1/2" with Philbe
design, $5-6; 2" flared custard, $3-4; 2 5/8" etched flower custard, $8-10; 2 5/8"
jelly jar (no design), $5-6.

Sunny Suzy baking set in original box, $75-100.

Nursing bottles: 8 oz., $18-20; 4 oz., $15-18;
Nip Cap, $150-175.

Two styles of Nip Cap, $150-175.

Sapphire Blue items (clockwise): handled mug, $20-25; metal coffepot with glass lid, $15-20; 4 1/4" individual pie baker, $18-20; 16 oz. measuring bowl (two styles), $20-25; 5 3/8" cereal bowl, $18-20.

Silex Dripolators. 6-cup, $125-150; 2-cup, $25-30.

6-cup Silex Dripolator with insert.

Fryrock blue deep dish. Scarce, $100+.

Sapphire Blue etched custards, $10-15.

Blue Bubble. Clockwise from left: platter, $15-18; grill plate, $18-20; dinner, $6-8; 6 3/4" salad plate, $4-5; cup/saucer, $4-5; 4 1/2" bowl, $10-12; 5 1/2" bowl, $10-12; 7 3/4" soup, $12-15; 8 3/8" serving bowl, $18-20; sugar, $20-25; creamer, $30-35.

Fire-King label on Bubble plate. Add $3-5.

Rare Bubble worker's experimental/lunchtime project, $200+.

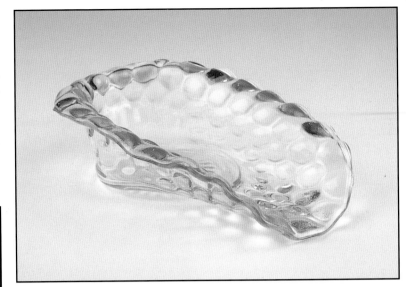

Go-along Bubble leaf dishes, $5-7 each.

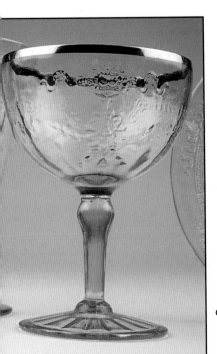

Philbe blue dinnerware. 8" lunch plate, $65-75; footed ice tea, $120-130; 9 oz. goblet, $200-250; 6" plate, $75-80.

Close-up of Philbe design.

Royal Ruby and Forest Green

This section includes a selection of Anchor Hocking's Royal Ruby and Forest Green dinnerware. For most of these items, we have seen no documentation to indicate that they were part of the Fire-King line per se. However, since these patterns were made in other colors that were marketed as Fire-King we have included them in this book. This is just a sampling of the pieces available. Whole books have been dedicated to Ruby Glass.

Royal Ruby and Forest green are readily available. Not surprisingly, they sell well at Christmas time. There are many sizes and styles of tumbler and goblets — too many for most collectors to need them all. Many of these tumblers were sold as promotional items or as containers for other products.

Royal Ruby dinnerware. 9 1/8" dinner, $10-12; 7 3/4" salad plate, $6-8; 6" plate, $3-4; creamer, $8-10; covered sugar, $12-15; cup/saucer, $6-8; 5 1/4" popcorn, $10-12; 7" flat soup, $10-12.

Royal Ruby 4000 line. 9" lunch plate, $10-12; 7" salad plate, $18-20; sugar, $6-8; creamer, $6-8; cup/saucer, $6-8; 6 1/2" soup, $20-25; 4 1/2" berry, $5-7; 8" vegetable, $20-25.

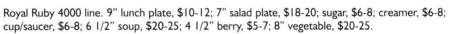

Royal Ruby Charm dinnerware. 7 1/2" salad bowl, $25-30; 8 3/8" plate, $10-12; cup/saucer, $6-8; 4 3/4" bowl, $6-8.

Ruby Bubble. Tidbit tray, $25-30; 9 3/8" dinner, $18-20; pitcher, $45-50; 12 oz. tumbler, $10-12; 6 oz. tumbler, $8-10; 8 oz, $10-12; sherbet, $8-10; 9 oz. goblet, $10-12; cocktail, $8-10; 8 3/8" bowl, $20-25; cup/saucer, $10-12.

Crystal pitcher, $10-12; Ruby pitcher, $100-125.

Ruby footed tumbler, $12-15; beaded bowl, $20-25; ribbed and garland bowl, $20-25; pitcher, $100-125; chimney, $20-25; large tumbler, $15-18; hand-painted vase, $12-15.

Ruby covered sugar, $12-15; creamer, $8-10; creamer plain handle, $12-15; sugar plain handle, $12-15.

Ruby and crystal lazy Susan, $50-60.

Ruby "Moskeeto-Lites"/ Vases, $12-15. Original box, $20-25.

Ruby Punch set: Bowl, $30-35; base, $30-35; punch cups, $2-3 ea. Forest Green Punch set: Bowl, $20-25; base, $30-35; punch cups, $2-3 ea.

Forest Green Bubble: 9 3/8" dinner, $18-20; 6 3/4" plate, $12-15; water goblet, $8-10; sherbet, $6-8; cup/saucer, $8-10; creamer, $8-10; sugar, $8-10; cocktail, $6-8; 4 1/2" bowl, $8-10; 8 3/8" bowl, $18-20.

Original box for Forest Green Bubble, $15-20.

Bubble candles, $30-35 pair; crystal, $12-15 pair.

Forest Green Charm. 11" platter, $20-25; 9 1/4" dinner, $20-25; 8 3/8" lunch plate, $8-10; creamer, $6-8; sugar, $6-8; cup/saucer, $6-8; 6 1/2" salad, $8-10; 4 3/4" dessert bowl, $5-7; 6" soup bowl, $20-25; 7 3/8" serving bowl, $18-20.

Waterford lazy Susan, $40-45.

Beaded-edge mixing bowl set, $40-45.

Forest Green tumbler, $6-8 each. Original cartons, $5-10.

Forest Green and crystal lazy Susan, $30-35.

Forest Green Vaporizer, $40-50.

Decorated tumblers, $6-8; with lids, $8-10.

Crystal and Additional Items

This section includes a few of the crystal dinnerware patterns that have become most popular in recent years. It also includes a small percentage of the oven and kitchenware that can be found. This is an area that is not heavily collected. These items sell in the secondary market simply as useable products.

We have also included Laurel Grey in this section since there was not enough Fire-King grey to warrant its own section.

Crystal Bubble. 12" platter, $8-10; 9 3/8" dinner, $5-7; 6 3/4" plate, $2-3; pitcher, $40-50; go-along hurricane lamp, $20-25; cup/saucer, $3-4; go-along leaf dish, $4-5; 9 oz. tumbler, $5-6; 12 oz. ice tea, $10-12; juice tumbler, $5-6; creamer, $5-6; sugar, $5-6; candles, $12-15 pair; sherbet, $4-5; 4 1/2" fruit, $4-5; 7 3/4" flat soup, $5-6.

Bubble flat tumblers, $8-10.

Odd Bubble tumbler, $10-12.

Sheaves of Wheat. Juice tumbler, $12-15; dinner plate, $20-25; water tumbler, $15-18; cup/saucer, $8-10; 4 1/2" dessert bowl, $10-12.

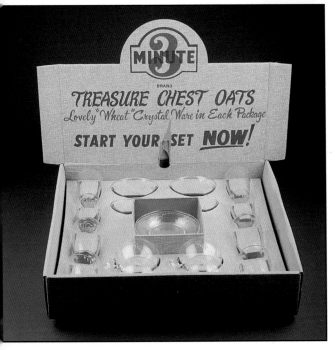

Original box for Sheaves of Wheat. Identifies the pattern name simply as "Wheat." $20-30.

Stars and Stripes. 8" plate, $18-20; sherbet, $12-15; tumbler, $40-45; go-along ashtray, $10-12.

Bi-centennial Eagle. Salad plate, $8-10; goblet, $6-8; cocktail shaker, $20-22.

Oyster and Pearl salad bowl, $18-20; handled candy, $6-8; decorated leaf plate, $4-6.

Crystal pitchers, $15-20 each.

Crystal pitchers. Etched, $15-20; pitcher with silver, $20-25; target ball jug, $20-25.

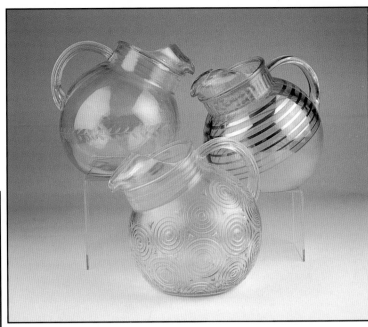

Etched pitcher, $15-20; pillar ball jug, $15. This item is being reproduced.

Decorated refreshment set, $30-35.

Crystal tumblers, $5-10 each.

Frosted pitchers. Large, $20-25; small, $15-20; tumbler, $4-5.

Splash Proof crystal mixing bowls, $35-40 set. Covered grease jar, $10-15.

Decorated grease jars, $15-20; with fired-on green, $45-50.

Ribbed kitchenware. Covered water jar, $15-20; large mixing bowl, $15-18; covered bowls/refrigerator jars, $10-15 each; 5" x 9" refrigerator jar, $15-20.

Crystal Restaurantware. Mugs, $8-10 each; cup, $5-7; bowls, $5-10 each.

Crystal Fire-King. Footed comport, $10-12; deviled egg tray, $8-10; mixing bowl set, $35-40; Bead and Bar pitcher, $20-25; ribbed butter, $18-20; crystal butter, $20-25; 4"x 8" leftover, $15-20; small casserole, $8-10.

START COLLECTING YOUR ENTIRE FIRE-KING SET TODAY

NEW FIRE-KING

TRADE MARK REG.

409—LOAF PAN
450—ROUND CAKE PAN
426—DEEP PIE DISH
422—CUSTARD
452—SQUARE CAKE PAN
408—CASSEROLE KNOB COVER
460—PIE PLATE
410—UTILITY BAKING PAN

Original Fire-King label.

Crystal ovenware, $5-7 each; measuring cups, $8-10 each.

Crystal ovenware set with original box, $30-35.

Fire-King ovenware brochure.

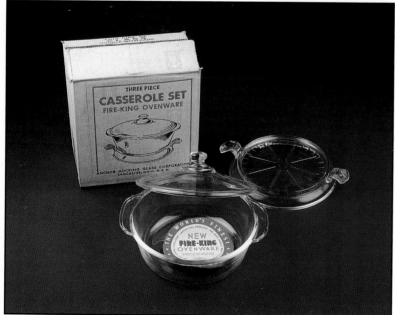

Casserole set with original box, $12-15.

Page from Anchor Hocking catalog.

Percolator tops, $2-3 each.

Decorated casserole, $15-18.

Gray Laurel dinnerware. 11" serving plate, $18-20; 9 1/8" dinner, $8-10; 7 3/4" salad plate, $5-7; 8 1/4" vegetable, $18-20; sugar, $6-8; creamer, $6-8; cup/saucer, $5-6; 4 7/8"dessert, $6-8; 7 5/8" soup, $12-15; go-along tumblers, $4-5 each.

Original boxed set of gray Laurel.

Fire-King 2000 – Reproductions

Jadite reproductions and new items have been appearing for the last four or five years. Despite Anchor Hocking officials' comments to us when we were writing our Jadite book in 1998 that Jadite would not be reproduced, an advertisement appeared in Restoration Hardware's Winter 2000 catalog that advertised and illustrated numerous Jadite Fire-King items that they were offering for sale. Printed over this section of the catalog was a notice that the first production of "Fire-King 2000" was rejected for poor quality. Restoration Hardware employees have since told us that they currently are not expecting to ever have these items for sale.

Some of the initial production has emerged on the secondary market via Anchor Hocking employees who got their hands on some of these items. All items that we have seen are poor quality and are marked "Fire-King 2000."

The items that offer the most concern to Jadite collectors are the Ball jug, which was to retail for around $25 and the crystal, covered butter that was to sell for around $12. We have not seen these items in the secondary market and do not know how or if they would be marked. Old ball jugs have no Fire-King markings.

Hopefully, this attempt to reproduce Jadite will not adversely affect the collecting of Jadite or the reputation of the corporation which created Fire-King.

In the spring of 2002, Anchor Hocking introduced a line of Jadite Fire-King ovenware that was produced for them in South America.

Fire-King 2000. Swirl mixing bowls, D-handled mug, small
bowl, dinner plate.

Fire-King 2000 Swirl mixing bowls.

Fire-King 2000 backstamp.

Fire-King 2000 D-handled mug.

Close-up of Fire-King 2000 label.

Index